FLYING FISHERIES BIOLOGIST

FLYING EXPERIENCES OF AN ALASKAN
FISHERIES BIOLOGIST

PRISTINE
PRESS AND MEDIA

Flying Fisheries Biologist
Copyright © 2025 by Kim Francisco

ISBN
978-1-964804-76-7 (Paperback)
978-1-964804-75-0 (eBook)
978-1-964804-77-4 (Hardcover)

This book is dedicated to all the people who helped follow my dream of flying and becoming a fisheries biologist. I can't name them all but my grandmother, mother, father, Sam Kavaugh, Dale, Mike Geiger, Bruce Hopkins, Lance Trasky, Ron Regnart, Bob, Mr. Cousins, Dick, Craig Whitmore, Dög, Mr. Sadler, Les Williams, and all of you whose names i've failed to list. I've been blessed to have a lot of wonderful people in my life.

TABLE OF CONTENTS

ACKNOWLEDGMENTS

First and foremost, my editor Florence Heacock. She improved the book enormously with her questions about content that required a lot of minor but essential rewrites. She also did an excellent job of cleaning up my final draft.

My technical editor was Ralph Alhouse, who, in addition to inspiring the book, checked the final draft for any technical errors in my descriptions of aircraft maneuvers.

The long list of people the book is dedicated to, who made it possible for me to fly, deserve more praise than I can give.

My dear departed wife Marsha, we didn't know it, was entering the final stages of frontal temporal dementia but still managed to remain supportive.

Lastly, my apologies to all the people above. I left out the Acknowledgements page in the first edition. The fault is entirely mine.

LIST OF FIGURES

PREFACE

If you read my first book, ALIBI MIKE and HIS GANG OF PARASITES ON THE STATE, thank you and you already know a great deal about me. Some have told me too much. This book is different, I didn't include the battling egos in my mind just one. This memoir covers my more memorable experiences flying. Mostly in small single engine general aviation aircraft, every now and then a larger plane enters. Most of the time I spent flying was safe and ordinary, it is the safest mode of travel after all. The many hours of doing the job and seeing Alaska were wonderful and I miss them. They also didn't make this book; you probably would have been bored silly.

I fell in love with flying at a young age and started flying lessons aftergraduating from high school. Then I became a fisheries biologist with the Alaska Department of Fish and Game for nearly 22 years. That job required a great deal of time flying, both point to point, commercially and more interestingly in the Alaska Bush in small single engine aircraft at low altitudes.

I now serve on a volunteer water quality, Rathbun Land& Water Alliance where I live in Iowa. I met and became friends with a wonderful gentleman Ralph Alhouse on that board and we were fond of swapping flying stories. Ralph, who is my senior and a member of the greatest generation started flying in the US Navy as a Kingfisher pilot in World War II. But continued flying in small general aviation planes the rest of his life. He finally had to quit in his 92cd year due to his failing eyesight. He told me several times I should write a book of my flying experiences. I finally did.

Figure 1Vought OS2U Kingfisher Courtesy
National Archives, photo no. 80- G-407853

PROLOGUE

Figure 2 Ford Trimotor Francisco Photo

As a child, like my friends I was fascinated with air planes and rockets.My father and I built model planes, plastic dust collectors, as my mothercalled them. Balsa wood and paper, rubber band powered free flight flying models were more interesting. Gas engine powered control-line modelscame next, but I got dizzy turning in circles with my control-line models so moved on to gas powered free-flight models. The constant repairs and total loss of models, that had many hours of construction in them and engines that took a big bite out of my lawnmowing/babysitting income discouraged my free-flight model ambitions. Then Dad and I discovered radio-controlled models. My mother was unhappy with the expense, some of which started coming out of the household budget, but Dad and I were hooked. We started small with a replica of the Cessna Skylane with throttle, rudder and elevator control. It was beautiful. Of course, Dad had to fly it first.

I successfully hand launched the plane and Dad guided it away climbing, descending, using the elevator and throttle controls. Then he made an 1800 turn. I warned him "Turn your back to the plane, like they told us." (They being the flyers at the local radio-controlled plane club.)

"I'm as good as those guys, I know the controls are reversed now," Dad replied.

Only seconds later as Dad tried to correct a drift off course, forgetting the controls were reversed, he over-controlled in the same direction as the drift. The Skyline's drift turned into a steep bank that resulted in what I would latter learn was an accelerated stall[1]. It dove straight into the ground, Dad's full throttle, full up elevator commands making things worse. The plane hit nose first, the wings survived but the plane's fuselage was destroyed. Dad lost interest in R.C. aircraft. He steered me towards model rockets after that, which also resulted in some interesting adventures and less expense.

During this model period, I noticed adds in the Des Moines Register for the big annual Ottumwa Fly-In. Restored antique and homebuilt aircraft from all over the United States, come to compete and have fun with fellow hobbyists. They have airshows to attract the public.

Ottumwa is a small city, eighty-six miles south and east of Des Moines. Ottumwa inherited a 1,440-acre airfield that was built and used during WWII as a naval pilot training center, which had become the home of the fly-in. No one could answer my question why the Navy chose a site about as far from an ocean as you can get.

By expressing frequently my desire to go (OK I whined a lot). I did convince Mom and Dad to make a family outing of a Saturday trip to the show. Not sure about how the rest of the family felt but I loved every minute except the constant restraint of waiting for the others. Someone brought a restored Ford Trimotor, an early entrant into commercial passenger aviation. They were offering rides, for twenty bucks, if memory serves correctly, that was a lot of money for the family in those days. I'm not certain, but I seem to recall my grandmother finally succumbed to my whines and I had my first flight in an airplane. I remember that it was really noisy, the three engines rattling the corrugated metal skin of the plane. I was surprised when we took off, I was sure I could pedal my bike that fast. We made a trip through the airport's landing pattern and set back down. I wanted to fly.

---

[1]   I wouldn't learn this until many years later when I was learning to fly and was taught how to avoid and recover from accelerated stalls.

NEXT FLIGHT

Figure 3 Cessna 140 by Robert Oehl courtesy Susan King

O ne Saturday afternoon, a few years later, I was fourteen or fifteen, I had finished my lawn mowing chores when Dad came from Sam's house next door and asked if I'd like to go for a plane ride. My flood of questions about who, what, when, and why were answered when Dad said "Sam offered to take us."

Sam had a private pilot's license and was renting a plane that afternoon and there was room for us. I never could figure out why it took Dad and Sam so long to get to the car. We drove out to Dodge Field, a small private plane strip a few miles from our house. Sam had rented a Cessna 140, a small taildragger that sat gleaming in the sun, its polished aluminum skin showing not a blemish. Sam took me (I think Dad was there.) on the preflight inspection explaining everything he was looking at and why. Then we climbed in, me first since I was in the rear "jump" seat. There was a notice on a placard on the rear bulkhead, DO NOT EXCEED 40LBS. I weighed at about 140. My mind did the simple math, as Sam and Dad took the front seats, and didn't like the answer.

"Sam, it says to put only forty pounds back here, I'm one forty."

"It's OK, I did the weight and balance, we'll be fine," Sam replied as he got busy with the starting checklist.

Huh, weight and balance, what's that? The engine noise pretty well made asking any more questions impossible. There was a hand grip on the back of Dad's front seat to make getting into and out of the plane easier. I grabbed it firmly, trying to redistribute as much weight as possible to the front seat. We took off. *I wonder how long I can hold on if my seat falls through the floor?*

It was fantastic. Sam flew back to our house where he made a turnabout a point, the wing pointing down at the house. Giving us a fantastic view of our two houses. Again, I loved the experience of flying. Sam and Dad didn't think so snice on the way home they teased me that Sam would have to pay damages for my fingerprints in the "chicken-bar."

All through junior and high school, flying stayed in my mind. I completed my flying merit badge while getting Eagle Scout. I read every book and magazine article I could find on flying and dreamed of getting a pilot's license.

MY FIRST SOLO FLIGHT

Figure 4Cessna 150 Ron Smith

The summer after I graduated from high school, my freshman year college tuition was in the bank, thanks to the three part-time jobs I held during my senior year. I had also managed to volunteer as help for a veterinarian since that was my professional goal. (Looking back, I don't know how I did it all.) One day, while reading a flying magazine, I saw a coupon Cesena had published for a free introductory flying lesson. Coupon in hand, I was on my way to Dodge Field, the nearest Cessna dealer. I decided to volunteer to be a line boy, the path many of the pilots I read about used to get their license. I was going to quit at least one of my jobs to fit it all in, if I had too.

Dodge Field wasn't much of an airport. I had been there the day we flew with Sam and it hadn't changed. The Iowa Aviation office was in a lean-to bump out from one of the hangers. Otherwise it was a narrow strip of grass surrounded by cornfields, with an even narrower strip of asphalt down the center of the grass. This was the airfield's single north-south runway.

Behind the office counter, two or three men were having coffee and I stepped up with my free lesson coupon in my hand. "I have a coupon for a free flying lesson from Cessna."

A dark-haired middle-aged man left his chair and with his hand out said, "Hi, I'm Dale, I'll take that. You ready to fly?"

I was taken by surprise, figured they be so busy I would have to schedule an appointment. Taking his hand, I introduced myself, "Hi I'm Kim Francisco. Ah, I have to be to work in a couple of hours."

"Great, you have plenty of time then. Follow me."

We stepped out the door opposite the one I had entered and back out into a bright, hot, muggy Iowa summer's day. An airplane, similar in size to the Cessna 140 Sam had rented, sat outside the door. Instead of sitting on its wheels and tail, this plane had a third wheel under its nose so the tail was in the air, like most of the larger planes I had seen on TV and movies. It was painted white with yellow trim instead of a polished aluminum skin. Dale asked as we walked, "Have you flown before?"

"I've been for a ride in a Ford Trimotor and a Cessna 140."

"Wow! Where did you manage to get into a Trimotor?"

"Over at the Ottumwa Airshow."

"Yeah, that's quite the collection of planes. This is a Cessna 150, we'll be flying in it today. It replaced the 140, with most runway's paved these days people wanted tricycle gear instead of the old taildraggers. Before every flight, it's the pilot's responsibility to do a walk-a-round and inspect the plane. There's no pulling over to the side of the road up there in the sky."

Dale proceeded to take me through the walk-a-round explaining what we were looking at and why. While he was at it, he was also doing a good job selling the airplane. I was hooked and landed before we strapped in. I wasn't use, to being treated as an adult. The first lesson was about 45 minutes of flight time with the 10 on the ground making an hour. I learned how to bank and coordinate turning the plane during that first flight. For reasons best explained by an aeronautical engineer, when the alerions on the wings begin a bank (turn) the nose points off in the opposite direction of the turn. If you hold the bank, it comes back but your turn goes more smoothly if you apply some rudder to swing the nose in the direction your turning. The trick is learning how much you need to push down on the rudder pedal with your foot so the turn is coordinated. Too much and the nose goes too far, causing the plane to side sideways. Not enough and your nose swings the wrong way, then back, causing a sloppy looking and feeling turn. At the same time, you also must apply back pressure to the yoke (steering wheel if you're a ground pounder) since plane's nose down and lose altitude during banks if you don't.

I'm not very well coordinated myself so was pleasantly surprised to discover I caught right on to banking the plane to the right and left while maintaining my altitude. *Flying is easy. Maybe I finally found something I can do well.* Luckily, I didn't say anything out loud. I left Iowa Aviation that day walking about six feet off the ground. They hadn't needed anyone to wash planes but I still scheduled my second lesson and pretty well emptied my checking account paying for the ground school supplies; a book, and flight calculator. Flight calculators are round slide-rules with various lines labeled for common calculations required before and during a flight, which I found simple to operate. (I always had a great deal of trouble using straight slide-rules and never understood why they weren't all round, which seemed simpler.).

My mother wasn't too sure about my flying but as long as my tuition was in the bank and I continued saving ten percent of everything I earned, Dad was all for it.

My free time was now spent learning the ground school materials, which covered flying techniques, weight& balance, navigation; both dead reckoning and radio, weather, and regulations. Sam and Dale had to answer a lot of questions.

I still couldn't afford to fly as often as Dale thought I needed. I had found taking off, apply power and keep the plane pointed down the runway, and flying easy. Landing was impossible, I thought. The ground rushing up just terrified me. I would discover that I had no depth perception. (Actually, nobody does beyond about 20 feet, our eyes just aren't far enough apart. Most people's minds pick-up the slack learning to judge distance based on comparing things they aren't even aware they were noticing. Some of us have trouble "learning" how to judge distance.) Most people solo, fly without an instructor, after about ten hours of dual time. Dual time costs more than solo since you have pay the instructor and rent the plane. I was starting to think I wasn't going to make it. Dale and I spent what seemed like forever flying touch and goes, taking off flying around the pattern (planes fly a set pattern around the airfield so approaching and departing planes can anticipate the location of traffic) then landing but not coming to a full stop rather once the nose wheel touches the ground you add power and take off again. I don't know how many touch and goes Dale and I did but he had to keep saving me.

My big problem was the flare. That is, you pull back on the nose of the plane raising it and the wings to a steep enough angle that the plane stalls. Quits flying, the engine is still running but if the wing is so steep that the air flow is no longer smooth, the wing stops flying. The trick is to judge your distance above the runway and make the plane stop flying just as you are touching the runway. Too high the plane will bounce; you can easily lose control and crash. Way to high and you'll blow the tires or collapse the landing gear, you crash. If you flare too late, you fly into the ground, which is another way of crashing. Student pilots learn the full stall landing first, simplest and safest. The "wheel-landing" comes later. It's smoother but you do fly the plane to the ground and it's harder for most people.

Since I didn't seem to be getting "it" with his help on the dual controls, Dale choose to let me learn from my mistakes. As long as I wasn't so high or low that I would kill us. He didn't tell me this at the time. I figured it out on reflection.

The 150 has spring steel landing gear designed to take a lot of punishment. Being "afraid of the ground", I tended to come in high. My landings were hard bounces that threatened to launch us out of control into the air. Fortunately, the plane usually stayed on the runway or close enough that my jamming the yoke into my stomach to keep the delicate nose wheel off the ground kept us alive and the plane in one piece.

"Watch your altitude," Dale reminded me as I made a final approach.

Too low for the altimeter. Scan wings. Level. Height looks right. Flare. We're falling too far. Should I lower nose and go around?

WHAM!

The plane groaned as the steel arms of the main gear squatted, threatening to let the belly of the fuselage scrap the ground. Then the arms snapped back to their normal shape, launching the 150 back into the air. As we rose the plane tilted to the left, with the yoke still in my guts, I added right alerion and rudder to correct the tilt. A plane's control surfaces wouldn't work because of the stall, which stopped the airflow over them., it continued tilting left towards disaster!

What do I do? Lower the nose.

I pushed the yoke gently forward. The nose dropped. Our air speed increased slightly, enough for the controls to level the wings. Our air speed was still low enough that as we reached the top of our bounce, we sank back to the ground, the main gear hit the runway again.

GROAN!

We bounced into the air but not so high or for as long. I had the controls neutralized except for holding the yoke back just enough to maintain the flare. The main gear once again hit the ground.

SREECH!

The motionless tires hit the runway, screeching as they dragged on the asphalt, their rotation trying to catch-up to the speed of the plane. It's a good thing the asphalt is black, so the long streak of rubber doesn't show.

As we slowed, the nose dropped and I followed the decreasing pressure on the elevator forward with the yoke. The nose wheel made a small, normal, screech as it touched down and began rolling. *Thank God we're alive!* I started to slump in my seat. *Brakes!* I sat-up straight to brake the plane to a stop.

Dale interrupted, "Time to go around."

Shit! I've had enough for one day. My new muscle memory taking over and I pushed the throttle in, added rudder to correct for the pull of the prop. We reached airspeed and I firmly pulled back on the yoke, first lifting the nose, followed by the main gear. Dropping the nose to gain airspeed but continuing the climb to pattern altitude.

We went around and to my surprise I pulled off a good landing. Dale sent me around two more times. I managed to repeat my performance. We called it a day. As I stood in a T-shirt drenched in sweat, Dale said, "Remember those last three. Try to do that every time and you'll be on your way to soloing."

I was feeling pretty good as we walked into the air-conditioned office, the cool air blasting my wet shirt made me shiver. The mechanic said, "I better go inspect that plane and see if we need to charge you for painting the belly." I tried to laugh along with the rest of the group but couldn't. *You dumb shit! You'll never be a pilot.*

*A week passed. Every time I thought of flying, I tried to follow Dale's advice and envision the good landings. My self-critic kept trying to relive all the times Dale had to take the controls, or ordered me to go around. I tried to force those memories out and remember my successes, though not always successfully. I arrived for my next lesson no more confident in my skills than I had been at the last. I almost gave up and didn't go.

I did the walk around, Dale joined me and we took off. "Kim take her around the pattern and do a touch and go," Dale told me as I climbed to 800 feet. Dread was building up as I turned final. *You can't do this. Give it up. Why humiliate yourself. Shut up! Just relax. Remember how those last three felt. What they looked like. Just do that again.*

"Nice. Let's go around and do that again," Dale said as I rolled down the runway. *I did it. Yes, now quit listening to your doubts and do it again.*

Two nice landings later Dale said, "Come to a full stop this time."
I braked the plane to a stop. *Wonder why he wants to see a take-off from a stop? I don't have any trouble with take-offs.* As the plane stopped. Dale unfastened his seat belt and dropped out the door.

"OK, you don't need me. Take her around and do three touch and goes."
The door closed and he walked away headed to the office. I sat staring at my hands on the yoke. Where's he going? I can't do this alone. I'll kill myself. Kim, he wouldn't have told you to solo if you couldn't do it. Do it.

Carefully going through the checklist and procedure for takeoff away I went. The takeoff was text book perfect. *Your flying by yourself! You're finally a pilot. You can do this.*

My landing was perfect. *We've got this now. Let's go.* I pushed the throttle in listening for the RPMs to increase.

COUGH, CHUG, PUTT, COUGH, SPIT, CHUG, PUTT!

What the hell! Check everything. My hands and eyes began checking everything, fuel tanks on, master switch on, mixture rich, throttle in. *Why isn't the engine running?* I pulled the throttle back. The chugging seemed to stop. I once again added throttle and the chugging resumed. *Check your location. Not enough runway left for takeoff, even if the engine could.*

I started braking. *Can't stop, going off end of runway. OK, we'll stop in the grass overrun. Can't slow down. Tires are skidding on the dew. Need more room. Do curves.* I began gently relieving pressure on one brake which caused the plane to skid left, then repeated to the right and back left. In spite of my curves lengthening the distance, the road's ditch grew increasingly closer, but the plane was slowing.

Can we turn around? Better not try, feels like we could roll the plane. Think we got this with the curves. Shut down just in case.

Thinking of the possibility of fire, my hands went through the engine shutdown procedure, while my feet steered the plane. Mixture lean, master switch off, fuel tanks off. The plane was almost stopped. Looking over the nose all I could see was road embankment but the plane was stopped. *Wow! Nosewheel must be right on the edge.* There was a slow final motion as the nose rolled into the ditch. *STOP, STIOP, O shit.* I found myself staring into the bottom of the ditch.

I leaned forward, pushing the yoke all the way to the panel and rested my head on top of the panel. *Why me. Thought I finally made it. I'll never be a pilot.* My self-pity was interrupted as the door popped open and a breathless Dale gasped out "Are you alright?"

I lifted my head. *No but that's not what he means.* "Yeah, I'm sorry. I did everything I could but the engine just wouldn't go." Other people were arriving now. All milling around behind Dale except the mechanic who lay flat on the ground at the bottom of the ditch, looking under the nose after running his hands down both blades of the prop.

Dale asked "Were those S turns when you were skidding on the grass your idea?"

"Yeah, I thought he was going to do a 180." One of the spectators said to no one and to everyone.

"I couldn't think of anything else to do when the I started sliding on that wet grass. Thought it would keep me out of the ditch." My voice trailed off in disappointment.

"Hey, you did great! We all heard the engine not catch, you got right on the brakes. Those S turns, when you started skidding in the grass, were inspired. Come on, let's get you in a plane."

Stepping out I could see the nose wheel folded under the plane. The mechanic was jumping to his feet dusting off his hands. "Crap. How much is this all going to cost me?" I asked.

"We have insurance, won't cost you a thing. You only folded the nose wheel. There're designed to do that. You did great kid. Plane all shut down and safe. Lucky that prop stopped horizontal. No damage at all. Now props, that's where the expensive damage is. Usually, when they run off the end of the runway, they leave the engine running. Bends the prop every time," he said as he continued his inspection looking into the cockpit. "Dale, he even turned off the master and the gas tanks. Nice job kid."

Can you do a nice job of crashing? That doesn't make any sense. Where we going? Dale had me by the arm leading me back at a quick pace. "Where you taking me?" I asked.

"Going to get you back in a plane. You're not done yet."

Fly! So, I can crash again! No way. "I can't today. Let's wait until next time," I said.

"Nope right now. If you don't fly now, you'll never fly again." Dale had opened the pilot's door of another 150 we had just reached. "In you go."

Say NO: don't get in. I was stepping into the cockpit. *Calm down. You can do this. The broken wheel wasn't your fault. Now buckle up.* Terror made me struggle with the buckles but done, I sat back to survey the panel and reached for the start-up check list.

"Hold on. Wait for me," Dale said from the just opened passenger door.

"OK," I said with a sigh of relief. Thought he was going to have me finish the solo.

I don't remember how many touch and goes we did, not many, perhaps only one. Dale climbed out and sent me on my solo again. This time the three touch and goes went perfectly. After parking the plane, I headed for the office drenched in sweat. The group gathered was silent as Dale signed me off as a pilot in my log book. Then everyone congratulated me with handshakes and back slaps. There probably were only three or four people but it seemed like a huge crowd to me.

Dale reached under the counter and came-up with a pair of big scissors, walking around behind me he said, "One more thing to do." As he pulled out my shirttail.

"Wait! This is a good shirt. I'll wear an old one next time." Should have saved my breath as he had the shirttail cut off before I finished. I signed my name, with some difficultly, the sweat wet fabric didn't want to take the magic marker ink. Dale dated, and initialed, then thumbtacked it to his trophy wall with his others.

I planned and flew a dual, then solo cross-country flights that summer. Then I was off to Kansas State University for my freshman year in prevet medicine.w

COLLEGE

Figure 5USAFROTC logo US Air Force

I**signed up for U, S.** Air Force ROTC. I thought they would let me continue work on my pilot's license, wasn't everyone in the Air Force a pilot? I was a preveterinary major at the time and the Air Force was looking for veterinarians, a surprise to me. During the second semester they offered me a full scholarship plus summer stipend in exchange for eight years' service after graduation. They wouldn't promise a pilot's license. I wrestled with signing the contract for a week. Potentially, depending on how long it took to get into veterinary school, I was looking at five to eight more years in college. With the Air Force paying tuition, I could use the stipend to fly. Eight years in service meant the contract was for the next fifteen or sixteen years of my life. I was eighteen, don't remember my first three years. This contract covered a period of time as long as I remembered living, probably longer since I think it was my fifth birthday when Mom and Dad rented the pony. One of my earliest memories.

I was also having second thoughts about veterinary medicine. I had volunteered as a vet's assistant during my senior year of high school, when I wasn't in school, working or flying. I loved the work, but my mentor had been pretty discouraging about taking it on as a career. The Air Force contract brought everything to a head, without a guarantee to fly, I opted not to sign and made my freshman year my last year majoring in pre-veterinary medicine.

I transferred from Kansas State University back home to Grandview Junior College that fall. Flying took a back seat. Between college, my jobs, and trying to solve the mystery of women there just wasn't much time or money for flying.

A biology major looking for direction. I dug out a career-day essay from my senior year in high school, where I had described three pathways to occupations. Substituting some new research, I replaced fur farming with aviation. Applied to three universities that had different majors in fields of interest to me. One was in Illinois, that had a major where you learned to fly, learned to manage airports, and several other skills useful to making a career in the flying industry. I also applied to the University of Alaska as a Wildlife Management major. The third was Missouri as prevet, that dream still haunted me. Applications in the mail, I relaxed confident that my rejection at two would determine my direction in life.

Life is never that easy. I was accepted by all three. Success can be disheartening. Luckily, one of my best friends from high school, Dennis Anderson, was also accepted by the University of Alaska. We made plans for an adventure filled drive to Fairbanks. Our plan was abruptly ended when Dennis received his draft notice. He went to the nearest Navy recruiter and signed up, following in our fathers' footsteps. Another friend, Dave Hayward, decided to transfer to the University of Alaska so everything worked out, except I had no money for flying.

I started working for the Alaska Department of Fish and Game in the summers, which included a lot of flying as a passenger. (See ALIBI MIKE and his Gang of Parasites on the State.) In the fall of 1974, my employment as a seasonal employee for the Commercial Fisheries Division of ADF&G was in its final days. My fiancé and I had planned our marriage for the weekend after my last day. Ron Regnart, Regional Supervisor for the Arctic-Yukon- Kuskokwim Region, gave me a call. "Kim, I haven't filled the research position for the pipeline[2]. I need somebody to go out with Bendock, from Sportfish Division, and count Coho salmon in the clearwater rivers running into the Tanana River for a couple of weeks. Can you stay on and do it?"

"Yes, Bendock and I are old buddies from tagging chums in Rampart. Marsha and I need the money," I blurted out. After a weekend as a married couple, we took our parents to McKinley National Park (now correctly Denali). The rest of my honeymoon was spent with Bendock. The couple of weeks helping turning into a twenty-two-year career (forty-five and counting on the marriage) as a fisheries biologist.

---

[2]   The Trans Alaska Pipeline, construction had just started and at that time pipeline had only one meaning in Alaska.

LEARNING TO COUNT SALMON

Figure 6. H-250Heliocourie by FlugKer 2
CCBY-A3.0 https://creativecommons.org/licenses/by-sa/3.0

The **Heliocourier dove towards a** large clear pool in the Porcupine River, banking to the right, so Lance in the passenger, seat would have a clear view of the fall chum salmon schooled up below. I slid across the rear passenger seat to look out the right rear window so I could see and count. We were so close to water and ground that I was a little scared. As were the salmon in the pool, they broke out of their school scattering, mainly upstream. I counted as quickly as I could. As we turned, the automatic leading-edge slats deployed with an unnerving "bang" to this inexperienced passenger. This was my first flight in a Helio, although

I had heard Fred Anderson raving to other biologists what an improvement it was over flying surveys in a Super Cub. As we took another bend of the river, Bob the pilot quickly corrected from a left bank back to a right bank, causing the four slats that gave this STOL, (Short Take Off& Landing) plane its ability not to stall in slow flight, too pop in and out. At 500 feet, even though we were flying only fifty mph, the gravel bars, water, and the spruce forest edge whizzed by at a frightening speed. I concentrated on counting the scattering chum salmon into my hand-held tape recorder. Suddenly Bob climbed, turned, studying a gravel bar out his window as it went past. His experience hands retrimmed the controls from slow to normal flight. He looked over at Lance saying something into the headset. Damn wish the intercom system included three headsets.

Lance turned his head back to me shouting, "Tighten your seatbelt. We're going to land and get those carcasses."

I had been busy watching living fish and had missed the gravel bar covered with salmon carcasses, which was really the reason I was with Lance to help sample carcasses. Getting my first lesson in aerial salmon surveys was a bonus. Bob turned into a short final approach, throttled back, descended rapidly, from my window in the rear seat it looked like we were setting down in the river. Adding a little power at the last moment, Bob gently set the plane down on the gravel bar. Then I thought we must be coming apart until I realized it was just the noise of the wheels throwing gravel on the aluminum skin of the plane. *Wow, now that's a real bush plane landing. Never did that before.*

The bar wasn't as flat as it looked and our rollout stopped at the top its highest point. The river looked awfully close, as I climbed out of the plane with our sampling kit, I looked at Bob and said "Nice landing, I couldn't decide if it was a full stall or wheel landing?"

"Couriers can't do full stall; they can't stall so they're all wheel landings. Are you a pilot?" Bob asked.

"I've soloed and have about twenty hours but finances haven't allowed finishing," I replied.

"A common story," Bob said, "flying is expensive."

Lance said "We're here to sample fish."

"OK, you want the forceps or the clip board?" I said.

"Clip board," Lance answered as I handed it to him. Taking the measuring tape and hooking the forceps over my shirt pocket where they would be handy, I noticed Bob doing a quick walk around the plane, checking for damage. Then he started walking back, following his wheel tracks. We, Lance and I, had reached our first carcass by then and I squatted down to measure the length. The scale came out really hard. Had to dig the tips of the forceps into the skin under the scale to pry it out. As I stuck it on the scale card, I said "Wow, these scales are really being reabsorbed.[3] Will they be readable?"

"Lots of them aren't, then we estimate the age based on length," Lance answered. That's part of the reason I sampled all those fish at the mouth of the river, those nice complete scales and the length would allow estimating age of unreadable scales by comparing length.

We stepped to the next carcass. As we worked our way, carcass by carcass up the bar, I noticed that Bob was pacing off very deliberately the length of the bar from water's edge to water's edge. He was also carefully

studying what was beyond the water at the upwind end. As a result, I wasn't completely surprised when we finished and he said, "This bar is shorter than I thought. Take off might be a little exciting but we can make it."

---

[3]   Pacific salmon stop feeding after they return to freshwater from the sea. They not only change color as they approach their spawning grounds but begin reabsorbing their scales. It maybe another source of energy besides their fat stores.

Lance said, "Are you sure? One of us could wait why you flew the other out."

Guess who'll wait. At least I'd get the front seat on the return flight.

"Nah, she can do it with all three," Bob said.

Bob taxied to the downwind end of the gravel bar, with engine out over the water, he locked one wheel with the brake, hit the power, the plane turned on the locked wheel creeping forward just a bit, we ended up with the tail wheel actually in the water. Bob held the plane with both brakes as he applied the throttle, even with locked brakes the wheels began to slide through the gravel, which was when Bob let the brakes off while finishing applying all 250 horse-power. We accelerated across the gravel bar, Bob lifted the tail as soon as possible to decrease drag and increase acceleration. With the nose down, I could see between Bob and Lance out the windscreen as the river rapidly approached. *Are we going to make it?* Lance braced himself, Bob concentrated on the scene ahead. Briefly, the noise of gravel hitting the skin stopped. Then started again as we finished crossing the river bumping up onto the gravel bar on the other side. Bob lifted the nose "Look back at the water?" Bob shouted. I looked back out my side window and could see a wake following our path dissipating in the river.

Bob said "I waterskied on the wheels across to the bar on the other side to finish takeoff."

Think I'll need a lot more experience before I try that! I leaned back in my seat as Bob circled so we could resume our count where we left off.

We overnighted in Fort Yukon that night. The fort, if there ever was one, is long gone. I helped Bob with the refueling while Lance checked us all in at the hotel. Bob and I talked flying. Me asking questions and he answering. My working future was a little uncertain at that moment. As we approached the hotel, I asked Bob, "I might get laid off soon, already stretched summer about as far as it goes. Could you guys use a line boy?"

"Maybe, but things slow down for us in the winter too. Drop off an application and we'll see," Bob said.

"What if I worked in exchange for flying lessons?" I asked. *Wonder how Marsha will feel about me being a kept man?*

"Good, cheap help is hard to come by, definitely stop by and we'll talk."

The hotel didn't amount to much, a large log building partitioned by plywood walls, steel bed frames (military surplus?) and an overhead single lightbulb dangled in the room. Lance and I roomed together, in the "James Arness suite." There was a picture of Mr. Arness towering over the shorter hotel owner at the front door. Pointing to it, I asked, "Lance did you have to pay extra to get Matt Dillon's room?"

"Huh," looking at the picture. "I'll be, wonder how he fit in the bed?"

Which, as I settled in, I discovered was a good question. I'm a half inch short of six feet, I always lie and say six, my feet were against the foot of the frame, and my head touching the wall. Didn't make any difference, I was tired and slept like a log.

Next morning on our way to the plane, we passed the liquor store. It was a windowless log cabin surrounded by an eight-foot chain link fence. The fence was about ten feet away from the walls. On the street side, the fence had two right angle turns that took it went right to both sides of the door frame. There was a small window with a shelf halfway up the door. To walk to the window, my shoulders would have brushed the fence on both sides all the way to the door. "Wow," I said "that must be Fort Yukon."

Laughing, Bob said "They have some pretty serious drinkers here."

We spent the rest of the day surveying and sampling carcasses. Not sure how many gravel bar landings we made during those two days, but they became old hat and I was ready to try one myself, but only if a skilled pilot was next to me.

WHAT I LEARNED
ABOUT HELOCOPTERS

Figure 7Awrospatiale Alouette II Marc Junker
courtesy Aerojet Helicopters

Looking down between my feet, I felt like I could see every one of the bright red Coho salmon with their black heads in the clearwater below me. I was counting steadily into my handheld tape recorder. Somewhere in the back of my mind, I was comparing this count to the one yesterday on the same river from a Super Cub. The fish were much easier to see and I was sure the count was more complete. This noisy rattletrap Alouette helicopter hadn't impressed me much when I first saw it but I was in love now. We reached the end of the index area; we don't count the whole stream just selected portions where salmon spawn annually. I switched off the tape recorder and gave the pilot thumbs up. He accelerated and climbed saying to me through the headset, "I hope we don't have to do much more of that."

I looked at him and he was soaked in sweat I replied, "Why, what's wrong?"

"If the engine quits, we'll be dead!" He replied.

"I thought helos autorotated." (Gliding" in a helicopter.)

"The rotor is only going fast enough to autorotate if it's going over sixty or we have fifteen hundred feet of altitude," he informed me.

Didn't know that. Slow flight with the Cub is sixty. Eight hundred feet is enough to set up emergency landing. Starting not to look good for helos. "Thanks for the education. I didn't know. We'll do the next one at sixty. Next survey is Delta Clearwater. Here." I pointed to the navigation chart I was holding for him to see.

"Good. I can stop at Delta Camp and refuel," the pilot said.

Hmm, another black mark against helos, shortrange. I made a note on my survey map for latter.

Survey maps are Xeroxed copies of USGS topographic maps of the stream being surveyed with the index areas marked and numbered. They often have been copied many times so were sometimes hard to read. We didn't use them for navigation. Index areas were important for several reasons. First, we assumed, not always true, that the salmon were distributed in a similar way from year-to-year. Index areas were comparable for spawning salmon abundance. When obvious changes, channel change, earthquake upheaval, or as my research found pipeline crossing occurred, we had to choose new index areas. They were also important for year-to-year comparisons because aerial surveys were highly dependent on water clarity. The downstream portions of a stream often could be obscured by high silt laden water following rainstorms. An annoying but necessary evil since this high water scrubbing of silt out of the gravel maintained the streams as good spawning habitat. The salmon themselves performed a similar chore when digging their nests, redds, with their tails.

Sorry, no equal pay for equal work among salmon. The female does all the work often leaving her with a raw wound where her tail had once had been. She helps the male defend the redd from other salmon until they mate, called gapping. As she lays her eggs, the male ejaculates into water flowing through the nest. They both open their mouths very widely, hence gapping is the name for their sex act, their bodies quiver with the strain of pushing out their sex product. They look like they're enjoying themselves. The first time I saw it, I was pleased that external fertilization looked like it was almost as much fun as internal.

Fairness between sexes doesn't get any better after gapping. It usually takes the female three or four efforts to expel all of her eggs. Fun over, the male moves on to the next female. The exhausted tailless and eggless female guards the redd for as long as she can hold her position in the current, a few days at most. Then she drifts downstream slowly succumbing to the effort, usually ending up on a bar to be sampled by everything from flies to passing biologists. While males do usually have a longer stream life, they also die childless. Leaving the next year's salmon to emerge from the gravel orphans.

As we flew the short distance to the Delta Pipeline camp, which was located at the confluence of the Tanana and Delta Rivers, I thought about my new-found knowledge about autorotation and helicopter safety. Might have to add a Table with the common copters' autorotation altitudes and speed.

Probably should check with Regnart and see whether this safety and cost per hour difference even make it worthwhile to continue the study. No, I shouldn't do that until I at least have a couple of comparable safe survey results to show him. Glad he taught me his style of surveying, 800 feet sure beats 500 that Lance preferred. Hey, it's almost lunch time. I spoke up to the pilot through the headset, "It's lunch time. You want to eat before we take off?"

"Never miss a meal, the grub is good at this camp. Excuse me, have to get on the radio," he replied.

The nearby Big Delta airport was an uncontrolled field as was the camp's helipad. He switched channels and announced our location and intentions for any other aircraft in the area. We swung over the warm springs (4 to 6 degrees Centigrade, 42 to 48 degrees Fahrenheit) not very warm unless its-40, at the confluence of the Delta River. This was also one of my study areas. The Delta was a glacial stream, a roaring torrent of silty, gray ice melt water, half mile wide in the summer. Now, in November, the glacial flow had ended and only the springs of crystal-clear water that never froze bubbled up out of the ground and fall chum and Coho salmon spawned in them. They were also part of the comparative study so we would do a survey after lunch. There were three spawning channels this year, the longest about half a mile so it would be brief at sixty. It was a short walk from the Trans Alaska Highway so we could compare surveys done on foot and from the two types of aircraft.

The Delta Pipeline Construction Camp was just across the highway. We set down at the helipad, connected the ground wire so a static spark wouldn't turn us into a flaming torch and pumped fuel into the copter. Then off to the mess hall. I took a short side trip to check-in at the manager's office. Part of the check-in protocol Bendock and I had learned the hard way when we violated it on our first visit.

After lunch, we did a quick survey of the Delta River springs. At a safe sixty, I couldn't see much difference with yesterday's survey with the Cub. I wouldn't really know until I transcribed tape and compared counts. We then flew upstream on the Tanana to the mouth of the Delta Clearwater River.

A much larger flowage also formed by upwelling springs but many more of them. It's about twenty miles long and navigable for most of its length. It wasn't glacial, so stayed crystal clear throughout the year except after really heavy rain. This would allow another double (triple?)

comparison since we conduct salmon escapement counts by air and boat on the Clearwater.

We started right at the mouth of the Clearwater where a few chums were still spawning. The chum salmon spawning was past its peak with only a few late arrivals still at it. For the next couple miles, it was just crystal-clear water and I saw the gray shapes of small fish darting about, whitefish or grayling probably. Then we started getting into small schools of Coho salmon migrating upstream so I became busy speaking numbers into my recorder. The Cohoes were approaching their peak of spawning so the migrating schools had turned into pairs defending clearly visible clean spots in the bottom where the female was digging the redd. My counting was mostly twos, fours, and various multiples of two depending on how may pairs were visible at once. Some pairs had attendants, males who hung around on the edge of the territory the nesting pair defended. Sometimes, I would see interactions when the attendant male got too close and the defender would charge and drive him off. Aerial surveys rarely gave you the chance to see actual dominance battles, you just weren't over the fish long enough. My observations from boats and on foot confirmed what the literature said; actual fights are rare and brief. Judging by some of the scars and injuries seen on carcasses some of the fights get pretty rough.

Flying at sixty, the twenty miles took about twenty minutes. I leaned back and stretched. I turned the headset intercom back on saying, "We can go home now. Done for the day."

Turning towards Fairbanks, the pilot asked, "I saw some people fishing, looks like it would be good?"

"Yeah, it's a premier Coho sportfishing spot this time of year. Blue Fox spoons with red or orange insert will catch one on every cast. Actually, anything red or orange works. If your use to ocean bright salmon, you'll probably want to catch and release. Meat quality of spawning salmon is not really good. They live on their fat and oil replacing it with water, red Cohoes don't taste too bad. They hold up better than most salmon," I replied.

"Might have to come down on my day off and try it."

"You'll have fun but it is cold out there, the eyes on your rod fill up with ice and your hands get cold, but the fishing is great," I told the pilot.

The results of helicopter and fixed wing counts of salmon escapement flown at "safe" speeds were virtually identical. I called Ron with the early results at the end of the fall chum/Coho salmon survey period. He wanted to continue the study into the king and summer chum counts the next summer to see if results continued to show the same pattern but told me to be ready to wrap the study up early if results continued to be the same.

My disappointment that one of my first efforts was probably a bust must have been evident in my voice. He told me, "Kim, null data is often the most important data collected. One of the biggest mistakes' researchers make is not reporting it. Then someone else wastes time and money getting the same answer."

Figure 8 Coho salmon in spawning colors Francisco Photo

BACK TO FLYING SCHOOL

Figure 9 Citabria 7EC Charlie Hall

The job continued to involve a lot of flying, to my satisfaction. Marsha and I were both working at good paying jobs, although our friends in pipeline construction were making unbelievably larger amounts. We managed to establish a house down payment savings account, continue the Cisco Permanent Fund, ten percent of everything we earned and reinvested. Still it seemed we had money to spend. We could have (should have?) increased the savings for a house down payment but peer pressure, seemed people at work either had planes or were getting them, lead me back to flight school.

The consensus at the morning coffee flying discussion was that if the plane wasn't a taildragger (conventional landing gear) it wasn't a bush plane. Instead of washing and waxing planes for Bob, I went to the Citabria (OK, American Champion) dealer. I talked to a long haired, breaded (just like me) instructor/salesman named Bruce Hopkins and soon went on my introductory flight in 115 HP Citabria. A tandem (passenger sits behind pilot), conventional landing gear, tube and fabric construction dream of an airplane. I once again was a student pilot.

Things progressed nicely. My earlier training came back; once again take offs and flying were easy, landings were still difficult. After another seemingly endless number of go-arounds, I just couldn't get a satisfactory landing set-up, Bruce's patience failed him and he gave me a dope slap from the back seat with his microphone. "Land the damn airplane, there was nothing wrong with that approach or the dozen before."

Guess it was what I needed. I finished going around through the pattern and finally did my touch and go. After enough touch and goes to satisfy Bruce that I was over whatever fear of landing I had developed, we stopped for the day. As he was signing my flight log, he said, "I think you finally whipped landings. Don't know what was bothering you. You're a good pilot."

"I have no idea what gremlin got into my head. Probably best if I don't think about it too much in case it comes back." I said. *Kim you're just a coward.*

Then he changed the subject and scheduled my next lesson at which predictably I soloed in the Citabria. I then progressed with my training. The "fear" of landing never returned, although, I did always consider landing the hardest part of flying.

A week or so later, I headed out on my first solo cross-country flight. I had planned my trip from Fairbanks to Delta Junction carefully. After Bruce approved the plan, I filed the flight plan and got the latest weather which included some high headwinds latter in the day. *Good, maybe they'll speed-up my trip home.* I fired up the plane and headed out uneventfully. Even though it was a familiar trip from my work, I dutifully logged the times to my checkpoints. I had way too many, danger of a familiar route, but it gave me something to do besides listen to the plane. Strange when your alone in a plane, there seem to be endless unfamiliar worrying noises that you hadn't noticed before. I logged in the Salcha River right on time according to my flight plan. I tuned in the local radio station and sat back and relaxed, enjoying the beautiful day. I began a day-dream about being a WWI pilot as I scanned the skies for Hun's, actually jets from Eielson Air Force base, one of my checkpoints on the route. I made a landmark check and I was still over the Salcha. *How's that possible. Time shows five minutes gone. Hmm, what's the getus.* I checked all the instruments, again, which I had been scanning regularly as part of my daydream. *Everything shows were moving at over ninety. Weird.* The Salcha wouldn't get behind me. I tuned the radio to the weather and got the latest forecast, the headwind forecast had been moved up. The ground school said winds varied with altitude, if you encounter headwinds change altitude. I tried higher, I tried lower, still the Salcha remained under me. *Have I entered the Twilight Zone?* I finally remembered someone describing a similar situation and they said they dropped to the deck, where the wind finally slacked-off enough to make progress. I reduced power to descend and the Salcha finally moved, behind me! *Just have to make this a strafing run.* I added power and lowered the nose beginning what should have been a power dive but the headwind held me pretty much motionless over the river in spite of my increased air speed and lower altitude, I did make it across the Salcha, but as I got lower the air turbulence increased to unbearable levels. *My ground speed is still practically nothing. To hell with this, I'm going home.* Making a climbing turn, I headed back to Fairbanks.

My landmarks whizzed by and I was in the pattern and on final in a quarter of my flight time out. Landing was a little tough. The wind had come-up so much that the plane wanted to fly without power, like a kite. My training was full stall landings, I thought the stall warning would never turn off, finally the plane set down, hard! We bounced into the air, I kept the stick back in stall, we came down again, hard, but this time we stuck. The turn for the taxi back was a little scary. The cross-wind wanted to turn the plane over. I managed to keep the wing down with the alerions although I think I made the turn on one wheel. Bruce and a mechanic ran out as I approached the parking area, grabbing the wing struts, I killed the engine and they pushed me into the parking area. *Geez, Kim, now they'll give you a set of training wheels.*

I jumped out to help tie down the plane saying, "I'm sorry, just can't handle this wind?"

"Not a problem, we had to help the two before you, too. Just too much wind." the mechanic said.

"Yeah, that was quite a landing. Thought you were going for three bounces. Next time we work on wheel landings," Bruce said as we walked into the shelter of the office.

"That's what you use in crosswinds, they work in high winds too?" I asked.

"They also keep you from landing backwards in high winds," Bruce added.

"O, did I bounce backwards?"

"Nah, almost though, your tough on the landing gear though," the mechanic added his concern.

"I'm sorry," a downhearted Kim said.

"Hey, we all bounce, should have seem my first landing on my instrument check ride. Three bounces. I looked at the guy grading me, "That's my three required landings," Bruce told me.

Laughing, I said "Did he pass you?"

"Yeah, but he said that since I was a smartass the first landing didn't count and made me do three more." Bruce answered, asking, "How was Delta?"

"Never made it. That wind stopped me at the Salcha and I used up my time trying to get past it. Didn't want anyone sending out a search party so I came back to stick to my flight plan," I said.

"Let's get you scheduled for wheel landings and another solo cross-country. Bruce replied. "You could save all this rental money if you buy a plane. I can make you a deal on that trainer?"

As I recall you were required to have forty hours of supervised, dual and solo, flying before you could take your private pilot's check ride. I thought I was going to use them all learning wheel landings. In theory their simple, you just fly the plane down to the ground as usual but instead of pulling back on the stick to stall, you just continue to lose altitude until you touch down. Then push the stick forward to keep the tail up and the main gear "glued" to the ground as you decelerate the tail slowly drops. Since your "flying" on the ground, the controls are still functional it allows you to hold the upwind wing down in a crosswind. After all the trouble I had mastering the full stall landing, doing the opposite action, pushing the stick forward, came really hard. I worried the plane's nose would plow into the ground. I was driving Bruce nuts, I think. He even hit me on the head with his microphone from the back seat again.

Luckily, I was doing survey work with Bob at the time, in a Helio Courier. They can't stall, well that's an exaggeration, but if you made a full stall landing the tail wheel would touchdown first and the plane would be nearly vertical. So, every landing is a wheel landing. When Bob heard of my troubles, he began teaching me to land the Courier. A bigger plane with twice as much horsepower and a yoke instead of a stick, but the extra practice helped. A virtually stall proof aircraft wouldn't land if habit caused you to pull back, so I was forced to do it right. I hope I didn't frighten Bob too much. I did, finally, master the wheel landing and came to prefer them. You always have control.

One day as I was returning to Fairbanks in the Citabria from my three stops, long solo cross-country, I was thinking of check ride to get my license that was scheduled for later in the week. Life was good. I called in my checkpoint as I approached the Fairbanks control area, also requesting the small plane runway. There was an unusually long silence before the tower asked me to repeat my location. *That's odd. Thought I used my best airline captain's voice.* I gave my new current location. I was given permission to enter the landing pattern instead of the usual request to announce when I reached a closer checkpoint. *I don't think he knows where I am.* I continued into the pattern getting ready to turn onto final for the small plane field when the tower ordered me to land on the main runway, which I was about to crossover. *What! Guess I can do that if I turn this into a short base leg and turn final now. Wonder what's wrong with the little field. Should I ask him to repeat? Nah, they get pissed off if you question them.* I jockeyed the plane around onto a short, crooked base leg then turned final. *Never landed on the main before. It's huge. Could do a crosswind landing perpendicular to the centerline, I think. Oh, SHIT!*

As I was descending, the hand of God suddenly grabbed the plane. The left wing dropped, it looked like the tip of it would smash into the runway. As the wing reached a ninety-degree angle to the runway, it finally responded to the corrective right alerion and power I was putting in. We rocked back into level flight, there was nothing but acres of runway in front of us so I pulled back on the power and landed. *I'm alive. Thank you, God. What the hell happened? Don't think he answer's flying questions. I want out of here.* With a racing heart I realized the taxiway was coming up, I turned left on to it. I didn't bother to ask the tower for taxi instructions. I just taxied the plane as fast as I could without taking off. If the tower called on the radio, I didn't hear. I was almost going too fast when I got to the parking area. I just barely got slowed down enough to make the turn and roll the plane into her slot. I tied down in a record time and don't really remember driving home. We didn't have a phone at the house so Bruce reached me at the office the next day.

"Kim, are you alright?"

Alright? What would be wrong. "Yes, I'm fine. Why wouldn't I be?"

"The way you left yesterday; we were worried. The controller should have never put you on the main runway right after that loaded Herc." (A Hercules, a large four engine cargo plane.)

"Is that why the plane flipped on my approach?"

"Yeah, those big planes put off wingtip vortices, they can spin a light plane like a top. You did great though. Told Al, you'd just make it into a victory roll but instead you recovered and landed."

"I still had plenty of runway." *Good to know I didn't screw-up.*

"Al went over and raised hell. Filed an official complaint for whatever good that will do. Their excuse was it was a trainee controller and he made a mistake. Do you want to go up before your check ride tomorrow?" Bruce asked.

"Nah, I'm OK. Guess I will need you to sign off on that last cross-country before I hand over my log book. I'll see you then."

"OK, see you then and you still owe us for the flight," Bruce replied.

The check ride went smoothly and I was a pilot, after I paid my bill.

TAYLORCRAFT BC-12

Figure 10 Kim& Marsha with Taylorcraft&
Toni Francisco Photo

One of the wildlife biologists was selling his Taylorcraft BC-12, a side by side two-seater. He needed a bigger plane for his family. The price was right and the bank loaned us the money. I became an airplane owner. When I told Bruce, he wanted to fly it since he had never flown one. I invited him out for a flight and supper. Once in the air, Bruce said, "I never gave you any spin recovery training. Let's try it."

He put the T-cart into an uncoordinated turn while pulling it up into a stall. The controls got mushy. The nose dropped and recovered from the stall, losing some altitude and we had a new heading but otherwise no big deal. Bruce held it in the stall and we went through two or three mushy stalls. The plane recovering by itself each time.

"Damn it. It won't spin. I'll fly it into a spin, then we'll practice recovery." He stalled again, with hard left rudder and right alerion. The T-cart kind of mushed over to the right but recovered, the controls remained mushy but functional.

"Damn it you're going to spin plane." He added power and began another series of stalling turns.

"Let's go home. She won't spin. Don't understand why?" Bruce said.

"The manual says that's one of the safety features is, it can't spin," I told him.

"Yeah, lots of manuals say that but this is the first time I found a plane its true for. Guess spin training will have to wait for your aerobatics course," Bruce, ever the salesman, replied.

AN INTERNATIONAL INCIDENT

Figure 11Pigs Mardsen A-Frane Acres
Courtesy Practicle Farmers of Iowa

The Trans Alaska Pipeline was nearing completion. My job on the JFWAT, Joint Fish& Wildlife Team, who monitored and advised on how construction would have the least impact on Alaska's fish and wildlife, was coming to an end. Al Carson, my JFWAT supervisor, (Ron Regnart was still my Commercial Fisheries supervisor, yes it was a strange arrangement.) was regularly busy taking various dignitaries on tours to show off the pipeline's special features. Most of all its elevated sections on special supports that allow it to slide back and forth as it gets longer and shorter, due to the flowing heated oil and changes in atmospheric temperatures. The elevation supports have passive heat dissipaters to keep them frozen in the permafrost. Otherwise, the changes in season would result in "frost jacking", which jacks supports out of the ground. Some of the elevated portions of the line, where animal trails were heavy, were raised above the normal height. Moose are tall, and needed the pipe higher to get under or as we called it "a higher BOP top", bottom of pipe, where you bopped your head. Some other portions were buried with refrigeration to keep the permafrost frozen in the caribou migration corridors. For some reason caribou cows were reluctant to cross under elevated portions thus requiring the buried refrigerated pipe.

Once meetings, vacations, and various other events aligned and all the JFWAT staff more important than me were unavailable to guide a group of mostly Soviet pipeline gawkers. It fell to me to be the tour guide. After some thought, I called Bob and was able to setup a charter for myself, the three Soviet engineers, I think, the fourth member of the group, the translator never made their positions clear.

They were impressed with the Helio Courier. We climbed in and picked up the pipeline just east of Fort Wainwright and began following it to the Delta Camp. I was pointing out various features over the headset to the translator, who then shouted what I said to the three Soviets in Russian. As we circled the Delta Camp, the translator asked if we could detour out away from the pipe. Guess they wanted to do some real sightseeing. I gave Bob a thumb's up and he began a sightseeing tour. He saw part of the Delta Bison herd in the distance. He pointed to the buffalo and nodded his head. I was running out of things to say so I nodded yes, Bob turned, and I explained what we were doing to the translator.

"We're going to look at a herd of American Bison. They aren't native to Alaska but several herds were established in the 1920s when it was believed they would become extinct with the loss of prairies in the main United States." I paused for the translator. When he finished, I added "They now support an annual hunt that is so popular we have to have a lottery for the permits every year." We had arrived over the bison. "There they are," I pointed out the windows.

We were at about 1,500' so the buffalo weren't disturbed, but our guests were. Quite a heated discussion started in Russian. The translator finally said "Those are pigs."

Is he kidding? "No, I assure you those are bison."

"PIGS! Why do you try and lie to us?" The translator shouted into the headset.

The discussion in Russian seemed very heated. *Now what do I do? I've started an international incident!* As I started to lean over the seat, hoping eye to eye contact might make me believable, my eyes met Bob's eyes, who was looking at me, with a mischievous grin. He pointed down with his index finger. *Good idea!* I nodded yes, and leaned back, checking my seat belt as I said "We'll go down for a closer look." Bob surprised me and the passengers as he added power doing a wingover and diving for the herd. There was silence, except for the roar of the engine as we dove down, pulling out twenty or thirty feet off the ground. Bob skillfully, quickly reconfigured the plane for slow flight as we approached then passed through the herd of buffalo. Sending them off in all directions. Bob started a turn for a second pass when a meek voice said over the intercom, "Yes, buffalo, not pigs." Laughing, Bob began a climb back to "tourist altitude."

When we got out in Fairbanks the group held a little huddle, while I waited at the truck. *Probably deciding who to report me too.*

The youngest in the group, the translator, approached me, shaking my hand, he said "That was the best tour yet. We really enjoyed buffalo. Thank you."

"Your very welcome. Better climb in we need to get you to the terminal for you flight to Dead Horse."

I drove them to the terminal on the other side of the airport. They grabbed their gear out of the back and we parted with handshakes and smiles all around. I drove back to the office wondering, *Pigs? How could they think buffs were pigs?*

Figure 12 Bison Courtesy Whiterock Conservancy

FLOATPLANES ARE ALSO BOATS

Figure 13 DeHavilland Beaver on floats. Ron Smith

Funding for JFWAT dried-up with the completion of the pipeline. Fred Anderson, Upper Yukon Area biologist for Commercial Fisheries, who I shared an office with had worked with, had become a friend. Marsha and I also owned one of his dog's puppies. Fred had been the assistant Area Biologist in Ketchikan, before transferring to Fairbanks. His old job opened up again. I had been promoted to a FB II so it would be a lateral transfer. I applied and interviewed with JPV, John Patrick Valentine, on the phone. I didn't feel like JPV had been impressed so I was surprised when a few days later he called and asked if I was still interested. Neither John nor Fred ever mentioned it, but I suspect Fred helped out. Who knows, maybe I was more impressive than I thought or the only applicant.

I found myself busy wrapping-up one job and planning a move. The T-cart was a particular problem. Paying to have the floats shipped to Ketchikan, would blow most of the small budget we were being allowed for the move. The float pond was still frozen in Fairbanks so I didn't have my float rating yet. I could fit the wheels into a trailer behind the car for the ferry trip to Ketchikan but that left the plane on skies with a pair of floats in Fairbanks. I was talking to friends, mechanics, and Bruce about working some arrangement that would eventually get the plane and floats to Ketchikan.

It was like wrestling with the old riddle about the man with the fox, chicken, and bag of grain, who needed to cross a river with a boat that only had room for one passenger at a time. My math teacher in high school hadn't cared for my answer; build a fire and cook the chicken. After lunch, skin the fox, then continue the trip with stops at the fur buyer and flour mill.

During my search for a solution to my new problem, couldn't cook the floats. I talked to an aircraft mechanic who told me that the Taylorcraft had a wooden main spar in the wing and it would wrap in Ketchikan's wet climate. I called John who knew about flying aerial surveys to count salmon but his knowledge of planes pretty much ended there. After checking with a number of people in Fairbanks, none of whom corrected the mechanic's information, I sold the plane. In retrospect, I wish I had asked John for the number of the pilot who they flew with, I would have found out there were Taylorcrafts all over southeast Alaska.

I spent a busy summer, learning how the new ocean-based salmon fisheries were managed in the Ketchikan Area. We shifted gears into the winter bait herring fishery. The winter bait herring fishery in Ketchikan was one of the oldest Alaskan commercial fisheries. It provided the bait for the longline fisheries for halibut and sablefish and more recently crab fisheries. When I first arrived, it was a neat and orderly fishery. Each cold storage, fish processors, who bought high quality iced or frozen salmon, halibut, sablefish, and crab from commercial fishers wanted a source of herring to keep frozen to sell or exchange with the fishers who delivered fish to them. To this end, they contracted a single seine vessel per company that went out and caught herring until the harvest guideline was reached that winter. I was surprised that competition hadn't caused more boats to enter the fishery; the usual pattern in commercial fishing. John, the Area Biologist.; explained there was a "gentlemen's agreement" between the companies that a slow harvest which maintained quality was more important than speed.

Bob, the other assistant was out on the RV Sundance, the seventy-foot research vessel assigned to the Ketchikan Area, doing hydroacoustic herring biomass surveys. It was my turn to be the office assistant helping John field calls and keeping track of the catch reports coming in from the cold storages. As the new guy, I was almost unnecessary since Michele, Office Administrator, and John already had a pretty successful system worked out. I tried to make myself useful, if they both were already on the phone or radio, I would take care of walk-ins or third calls.

One morning, John suddenly came out of his office and said "It's over, Icicle just took the last of the guideline. Michelle, do a news release announcing the closure at 3:00 PM today. Kim, start calling all the processors with the closure." He turned to go into his office muttering to himself "Need to call Juneau, write emergency order…" and he was out of earshot. John was an interesting guy, his mind was totally occupied by the job, until it was done. I got on my phone with the news.

Things went well. We all got our assigned tasks done. Michele was busy at the copy machine making copies of the news-rerelease for me to deliver around town. She would FAX copies to the press and processors located out of town. John came out of his office visibly upset. "Phillip's (one of the cold storages) just called. Joe is up Behm Canal. They can't reach him on the radio. Kim, he's on the Board of Fish and Game, we have to keep him from fishing illegally. Dick is teaching (Our regular pilot.).

Call around and see if you can charter a plane to take you up there and find Joe."

"OK." I went to work on the phone. Finding a plane to charter proved difficult on such short notice. When I called Webber Air I lucked out. The senior pilot happened to be standing next to the dispatcher and overheard her telling me they didn't have any pilots or planes available until tomorrow. He took the phone, "What do you need to do? It's too early for salmon surveys."

"I need to fly Behm Canal and find a herring boat that doesn't know the fishery is over."

"Got a Beaver we just finished swapping engines on. Get right down here we'll do the test flight and your charter."

"Great. I'll be there in five minutes." I answered.

He hung-up. I jumped up grabbed a news release and headed towards the door, telling Michele "I'll be flying with Webber looking for Joe. Not sure how long it will take."

On the short walk to Webber, I started thinking How safe is taking the test flight in a plane they just "swapped engines "out of and into. Remember that plane in Canada that started its takeoff and the engine flew off into the lake. Plane sat on its tail but it floated. Exciting but safe. Heard the mechanic forgot to tighten firewall bolts. But if it happened after it was airborne!

I arrived and walked up to the desk. An older pilot was behind the desk with the dispatcher when I introduced myself. "OK, let's see if we can lend a hand getting the plane in the water," the pilot said after shaking hands.

I followed him into the hanger area which usually was out of bounds to nonemployees. Most of the hanger was built on a wooden deck on pilings over the water. As we walked in, we went past a Pratt& Whitney Wasp radial engine on a stand that was being either disassembled or reassembled.

"Is that the old engine?" I asked.

"Nah, that one we finished. It will go out next. The old one is there." He pointed to an engine on another stand that appeared to only be missing the plane. "With this fleet of Beavers, we're constantly rebuilding engines so we can swap 'em out. Here's ours." A mechanic was finishing buttoning up the engine cover on a Beaver that seemed to tower over us, sitting on its floats on top of a big flat dolly.

"Is she ready?" the pilot asked.

"Yep, good to go. The kid even remembered the oil this time," was the answer.

"Yeah, he won't make that mistake again," the pilot answered. "Let's get her in the water. Grab a strut." I walked up to the plane and griped a float strut. We then pushed the plane over to an elevator in the deck/floor. The hanger's ocean side was missing. Instead there was a wonderful view of Tongass Narrows, and its plane, and boat traffic. We turned the plane on the dolly so it faced the narrows, and rested on a part of the floor, that was also an elevator. Then the elevator was lowered, putting the plane and dolly into the water. We climbed down a ladder to the dock below. Once the plane was afloat, we guided it off the dolly and tied it alongside the dock.

"Climb in." Following instructions, I climbed up into the co-pilot's seat. The pilot climbed into his seat. The line boy, wasn't really a boy but that's the title, held the plane. The pilot called "CLEAR" and started the engine. It ran smoothly being warm from its test run in the hanger. We pulled away from the dock. The pilot got on the radio announcing our presence and intentions to the tower and other pilots. Then he hit the power and the 450 horses roared to life. The twenty odd year-old airframe shook and rattled as it squatted tail first towards the water. *Here's where the plane in Canada lost the engine.* My concern was unnecessary and the floats rose onto step, nose came down and the wings leveled, we lifted off. There was a low ceiling, the clouds were only at about 1000' preventing us from shortcutting over Revillagigedo Island to back part of Behm

Canal where the radio reception was blocked by the mountains. We took the scenic route following first the narrows then the canal to the east and north. Looking for Joe's distinctive black seiner. Normally, the views in Misty Fjords on the east side of the island are breathtaking. Today, it was shrouded in clouds and mist, which is why it's named Misty Fjords. Still beautiful, in a mysterious way.

This was taking longer than I thought. Beaver charters are rather expensive by the hour. The ceiling continued dropping, we descended to 200 feet. "There," I was finally able to point to Joe's boat resting quietly at anchor in a small bay on the northwest corner of Revillagigedo Island. We turned and buzzed the boat then landed, pulling up to the stern nose first. The pilot killed the engine, as we coasted up to the boat's stern. I dropped out onto the float on my side, grabbing its bowline from where it was dragging alongside in the water. I moved forward, luckily our buzz had the desired effect and the man on anchor watch came to the stern, catching the line I threw him. I took a couple steps back to the passenger door, looking in at the pilot as I grabbed the folder with the news release.

"You go ahead and jump on. Let the plane go. I'll just drift until you signal me," the pilot instructed.

"OK, shouldn't take long." I said.

I returned to the bow of the float, stuffed the folder into the front of my pants saying "Permission to come aboard." I didn't wait for an answer just took a jump getting my arms over the rail and my feet on the rub rail. The crewman on anchor watch grabbed the back of my coat and flopped me over the rail. I did manage to land on my feet, also my hands, not the greatest boarding. Standing, I asked, "Thanks, let the plane go, he'll drift. Is Joe awake?"

"Yes, no one could sleep through that plane," Joe answered smiling coming around the mast. He was a short broad, strongly built man. A middle-aged Tlingit, who I had met previously in the office, he had told me to call him Joe, but I still sprinkled sir into my conversation, since he was a man who deserved respect.

"Sorry to wake you. Did you have a good night sir?" I said.

"We got a few tons, but you didn't fly up here to ask about fishing?"

"No, the harvest guideline was taken last night. Neither Phillips nor we could raise you on the radio. John sent me up with the news release so you wouldn't go fishing after the closure at three this afternoon," I explained.

"That was thoughtful of John and you."

"Your welcome. Err, I have a copy of the news release if you want it, I said. I'm not good at small talk and was running out of topics."

"No, just make more trash. Kim, do I need to dump last night's fish? Joe asked.

"No sir, you can still deliver those. They were taken before the closure." Most of the crew had gathered around and were muttering their disappointment. The closure meant no more income since they worked for a shares of the gross.

Joe looked around saying, "Let's get underway. We can eat breakfast on the way to Ketchikan."

"Guess that's my cue to leave." I waved to the plane. "I'll see you in town, Joe," I said, he nodded and headed for the wheelhouse.

The Beaver started, taxied a short distance then the pilot killed the engine, coasting into the stern. I climbed over the rail. Standing on the rub rail, facing the water and plane, my hands behind me holding the rail. As the plane arrived, I reached out with one hand grabbing the prop hub. Then sort of stepped/fell off the boat on to the bow of the right float. It went under from the sudden weight and impact. I fell backwards, my shoulders bouncing off the boat. I had a bad moment as the plane drifted from the boat and I was trying not to fall off the float backwards. The pilot's grin didn't help the situation. I managed to stay on the float.

Grabbing the prop hub with one hand as I dipped a knee in the water sloshing over the float. Luckily, my boot found the cleat on the float's bow and I was able to regain my footing. If it hadn't been a Beaver, I would have gone for a swim, fortunately the big plane comes with big wide floats. I stood and walked back to the door feeling the fool. A glance back at the boat didn't show any spectators. The crew was busy winching up the anchor and with other tasks required for getting underway. Between the anchor winch pulling Joe's boat away, my push, and wind the plane quickly drifted away. We had a lot of space by the time I started buckling the seat belt/shoulder harness into place.

A still laughing pilot managed to ask, "Ready to go?"

"Yes, I think that's all the entertainment I have in me today," I answered.

Laughing, he started the engine and added throttle, we soon lifted off as we came alongside Joe's boat, the crew sending us off with waves. We didn't climb very high; the ceiling was only about 300'. Ketchikan was closer following the western arm of Behm Canal. We chose to finish circumnavigating the island. We continued flying above the canal steadily descending with the ceiling. The pilot called ahead for weather, the Ketchikan Airport and Tongass Narrows were below visual flight rules (VFR) which we were operating under. I asked, "Are we going to wait at one of the lodges?"

"Nah, I can get in under this shit," was the answer.

We continued, descending, closer and closer to the water. I couldn't see very far in front under the clouds. *This is getting a little scary. There are no old bold brush pilots. He's old, relax and learn.* Suddenly a boat's wheel house and boom reached up out of the mist for us. I jumped but the pilot didn't quiver.

He did say, "Time for a boat ride." He landed the plane straight ahead so we didn't lose any ground on our route. Also avoiding a dangerous low altitude, low visibility turn. We were almost to the entrance of the

Narrows, turning on all the lights, he radioed the tower that he had landed and we were taxiing to Weber Air.

"Do you do this often?" I asked.

"God no, this can be terrible for the prop. That's why we're going so slow. Spray just eats up props. Water is hard when it gets hit fast," he replied.

"Yeah, probably worse than a belly flop," I said.

"What's a belly flop?"

"You don't swim I take it," I said.

"Nope, born and raised here, waters too cold to learn. Course there is the pool now, but I've never been," He explained.

"A belly flop is when you go off the diving board and either screwup your dive or some people do it on purpose to splash others and you land on your belly. Like hitting pavement. Hurts like hell. Your skin turns red. Anyway, having done a few I can see how a prop might erode in spray. Never thought about it though. I'm hoping to replace my T-cart so that will be good to know," I said.

"You had a Taylorcraft, fine airplane. What happened to it?" he asked.

"I sold it when I transferred to Ketchikan," I said.

"Why the hell did you do that?" He asked.

"Mechanic in Fairbanks said the humidity here would warp the wooden main spar," I answered.

"What an idiot. Wouldn't let him work on my planes. There's T-carts all over southeast, their great little float planes. Never heard of a warped spar yet," he told me.

"Screwed-up again," I said. "Had floats and skis too. Wish I had talked to you. Couldn't find anyone in the office who knew planes."

"That's the hell of life, you have to make mistakes to figure it out," He said.

We completed a long taxi but finally made it back. As I came in the office John greeted me, "Did you find Joe?"

"Yes, I found Joe and he's on his way in with about four tons of herring. It took so long because of this terrible weather. We had to land out by Clover Pass and taxi the rest of the way in," I said.

"Good, you found Joe so he won't get caught fishing after the closure." John turned and went into his office. Michele was busy typing. *Guess flying in marginal weather is just what we do. Guess that's why the legislature put us on twenty-year retirement.*

Figure 14 Joe's seiner Francisco Photo

LUSCOMBE 8E

Figure 15 Luscombe 8 on floats from collection of Alan Radecki

We **became home owners for** the first time in Ketchikan, but we had been a little short for the house down payment, we borrowed the extra money from my brother-in-law. All our extra money went to paying off that loan as quickly as possible so I couldn't think about buying a plane for nine months. Although most charter pilots, as soon as they found out I was a pilot would let me fly. If the plane had dual controls, I still wanted a plane of my own.

Finally, with the down payment loan paid back, I started work on my floatplane rating with Mr. Cousins; "Watch out for the slippery green shit." Floatplane rating in hand, I started looking for a plane. Most were beyond my means but finally met a nice man who was selling his Luscombe 8E on floats for a price I could afford. He wanted to pay for his Instrument Flight Rules rating with the proceeds. The plane had a current annual inspection, the floats leaked a bit, most do, but otherwise it seemed OK.

I didn't have a mechanic check it out, as everyone advisees when buying a used plane. I knew what I was doing and the owner was a good guy and wouldn't rip me off.

I flew when I had a chance, but we were busy during the summer. Marsha didn't care for flying in small planes much so I was usually alone. Towards the end of summer, it was time for the annual inspection.

Dick Hamlin, our regular pilot, had a large hanger floating on a log raft. In exchange for cleaning-up part of the hanger, he let me put the Luscombe inside for the inspection. His regular mechanic was willing to let me do the busy work of the inspection; removing and replacing inspection plates and such.

As soon as I roared up the ramp into the hanger, Dick got a funny expression. I shut down the plane and climbed out. Dick was poking at the bottom of the floats with a screwdriver.

"Kim, these have been fiber-glassed!" He said. I crouched down next to him and looked.

"Is that a legal repair?"

"Nope. Looks like you're going to learn how to rivet floats." He chuckled. "You're going to be in here longer than I thought. We're going to have to talk about rent."

"Crap, wonder if Rich[4] knew when he sold it to me. Guess I should have had a mechanic inspect it. I at least should have gotten it out of the water so I could check the float bottoms. Fiberglass seems to work alright but not FAA approved," I moaned.

Dick and I pushed the plane right and left, working it over to the side of the hanger cleared for it. Dick left to pursue one of his many jobs; teaching math in high school, salvaging beach logs, charter flying, and

---

[4]   Made the name up. I don't remember it.

renting hanger space. I began the tedious job of removing the inspection panels. *Wonder if I reregister the plane as experimental if I can use fiberglass float bottoms? Have to look into that.*

I didn't find any new disasters as I pulled the panels and peeked into the exposed parts of the aircraft frame. Dick's mechanic showed up right as I took the last panel off.

"Fiberglass has to go. Then we can see if the floats just need new seals and rivets or if the damage is worse," was his opening remark.

Guess optimism isn't part of his trade. "Yeah, I've been poking at some of the edges with a screwdriver. I think it will peel right off," I said.

He was peering into the float access panels with a flashlight, shaking his head in the negative. "Don't see anything but fiberglass, you're going to need new bottoms."

I suppressed a giggle, inspired by fourth grade humor. *Hey this is serious. Going to run into money. Don't laugh.* "How much do they cost?" I finally asked.

"Depends on how bad it actually is when you get the glass off, new set of floats might be cheaper," Dr. Gloom said.

"Shit," a short reply but it covered everything.

"Let's start with the engine," He said climbing up onto a float so he could reach it better. I followed, taking the kitchen strainer he handed me. *Guess this is some of that high-tech inspection equipment they get paid so much to have.*

"I'm going to pull the oil drain, hold the strainer in the oil." He pulled the drain plug and oil flowed into the strainer and then the plastic bucket I was holding under it. A piece of metal, about an eighth of an inch square stopped in the strainer.

"That's not good," I said. Wow, just flew over here this morning, good thing engine didn't quit.

"That's not a big deal," Dr. Gloom said. "But this is." He finished as the strainer rapidly began filling with pieces of metal of various sizes and shapes. *How did this thing stay in the air the last couple of months?* The strainer filled to overflowing with metal shavings, pieces, and chunks.

"Hand me the strainer?" said Dr. Gloom.

"But the oils not done yet?" *That was stupid thing to say, all the new pieces are bouncing into the bucket.* I turned the handle to him and he took it. Looking closely at the oily pieces and poking through them with his finger, knocking the ones on top into the bucket of oil, where pieces of metal continued to make little splashes as they came out in the stream of oil.

"How did this thing keep running? "I asked.

Dr. Gloom looked at me saying, "These engines can fly with an amazing amount of damage. But they do quit, finally. Looks like that's all the oil. Do you want to go on or wait until you get the floats and engine rebuilt to finish? I'll only charge you for a half hour if we quit now."

"Yeah, let's call it a day. I'll have enough trouble explaining this to my wife," I said.

"A rebuild on this C-85 might be hard, parts are scarce. You might want to look into the Lycoming-125 conversion. A guy had one of these 8Es with that 125 horse and it was a screamer. Could land and takeoff of the smallest lakes." Dr. Gloom had some good news.

I did some checking around and finally found an overhaul shop in Kent, Washington that would do a rebuild on the C-85 for less than a 125 would cost. I crated it up and shipped it off to the shop. A month or so later my office phone rang, "Hello, Commercial Fish, "I answered.

"Mr. Francisco?"

"Yes."

"We have your Continental 85 here for a rebuild."

Great, how can it be worse than a total rebuild. Maybe it's done?

"Yep, that's mine. What's up?"

"Did you notice the data plate had been removed?"

"No, I could see where it was supposed to be but it looked painted over."

"No, it's gone. We discovered the reason is that the engine's serial number doesn't match the log book. Checked and it's on the list of stolen engines. We won't work on it. We are shipping it back to you COD. We're not the police so won't report it. It's your problem."

"Ugh, thanks, I guess."

"Good bye."

Doesn't sound very happy with me. Shit, what do I do now? Hot engine, what's the Federal penalty for receiving stolen goods? Try to sell it as a rebuild project but then I'm guilty of fencing stolen property. Plus, it's not the right thing to do. Not sure if I got much work done that afternoon as my mind churned over alternatives.

I resisted temptation and did the right thing. I called an acquaintance at the FAA, maybe should have called an attorney, but he listened to my hypothetical problem and gave me good advice instead of sending the police. When the engine arrived, I took the maintence log book and engine to the FAA and turned it in. Filled out a form explaining how I had come into possession of an engine that didn't match its log book and got a receipt for the engine. Then I waited, worrying. I finally received a phone call from the FAA, I verified the details of the sale to the investigator. Either he or a later caller told me the case was settled, I could pick-up the engine to sell for parts or they would junk it. I didn't want to see that crate full of engine again so left it to them.

The floats turned out to be a disaster. The main wing spar was suspect and should be magnifluxed, which would require disassembly of the wings. Imagine flying along and a wing breaks off! I gave up at this point. No sense in throwing more money into this hole in the sky! Dick's mechanic sent a guy to me who was looking for a project airplane. Getting this bird into the sky again was going to be a project exactly what he was looking for. I've forgotten the exact numbers but when I worked out what I had lost, at the request of my wife, I recovered about a third of my "investment." As I recall, I cheated just a bit on my report of what was spent. Left out little things, long distance phone calls, shipping, hanger rent, mechanic's bill, you know just little stuff that would have bored Marsha.

PICK YOUR PILOT

Figure 16 Crashed C-185 on floats ATSB photo

During the spring, I learned how to map herring spawn from the air and sample it underwater while scuba diving. Flying herring is safer than most of our survey work. There usually is plenty of room for the plane over the coast and we flew at a safe 1,200 ', which meant in the event of an engine failure or some other unexpected event the pilot had enough altitude to recover and set up a survivable crash landing. None of which happened.

Next John sent me out with our regular pilot, Dick Hamlin, for lessons in counting pink salmon, in schools seen in the ocean or in their clearwater spawning streams. There were two primary differences to my previous experience counting king and chum salmon; pinks are smaller and an order of magnitude more abundant. In their spawning colors, which close up is a dull gray or green back and a yellowish white belly. From 800 'they are a distinctive black and white. King salmon come in single digits, sometimes in tens, chum salmon come in tens and hundreds. Pinks almost always come in hundreds and often thousands.

When I first started counting fish from the air, I used a trick a former U2 pilot turned ornithologist had taught us for counting birds from the air in college. You throw some rice on a table, then take a quick look counting/ estimating the number of grains. Then you count them. Repeat until you get it right. Evidently, the technique works for salmon. I had to do some refresher training with rice to master pinks. Worked well, except for the rice that made it to the floor and I missed cleaning up. Marsha raised Cain.

Dick was a rare pilot who could fly and count. I think he still preferred an observer, so he could concentrate on flying but he would never admit it. After Dick told John I could count, I and the other assistant were doing a lot of flying with various flying services so we could cover more streams during our "weather windows." John trusted Dick so flew pretty exclusively with him.

We, a new to me pilot and I had just finished the last stream in Kasaan Bay. We were in a Cessna 185, on floats, crossing over a piece of Prince of Wales Island to Cholmondeley Sound. I was missing the scenery, being busy cleaning-up the survey notes on my clipboard. In southeast, they still "recorded" surveys on a clipboard with a photocopy of a map of the stream. My suggestion that we try handheld tape recorders, like in A-Y-K, wasn't even worthy of discussion in the staff meeting.

Suddenly, the engine's steady roar missed a beat. I looked up; the engine began running rough. I pulled my knees up, out of the way as the pilot's hands were busy checking engine and gas tank settings. A burst of smooth operation relieved us both, then with a cough and a backfire, the engine quit. The sudden silence was eerie.

"Shit," the pilot said as he trimmed the plane to its best rate of glide. *Lengthening our life expectancy.* His hands returned to engine controls as he went through an unsuccessful restart. The tall spruce and hemlock trees were reaching up for us. There wasn't a flat spot to be seen. It was all steep, craggy slopes covered with trees. What would normally be beautiful scenery was suddenly becoming the jaws of death, reaching up for the plane. I pulled my seat belt tight. *God please forgive my sins, intended and unintended. Please welcome me home.*

"Damn, missed the tank switch," the pilot said as he reached for the fuel tank switch between the seats. He switched from right to left. Started his restart routine, as we heard the first swishing sounds of the floats touching the tops of the trees. The engine roared to life pulling us up and away.

Thank you. My mood quickly went from being thankful and relaxed to anger. *I told him to switch to both tanks for surveys.* Most Cessna's have a three-way gas tank switch; right, both, left. This plane had such a switch. "We're done. Return to Ketchikan," I ordered.

"Hey, just forgot to switch tanks, could happen to anybody," the pilot said.

"I told you to use both tanks. I won't fly with you, you're not safe. We're done."

"But no harm was done. You just have a good story," the pilot pleaded.

"No. We're going back."

The pilot muttered and I fumed, at least halfway across Clarence Strait. Then my better nature and ethics started to get in the way. Kim, your alive, no reason to be so hard on the guy. You're supposed to be forgiving. He almost killed us. Yeah, but he almost killed himself. Remember what Regnart said "If a pilot ever makes you uncomfortable, don't fly with them. That's how to stay alive." Yes, but what about forgiveness? What about your life? I wrestled with my personal ethics the rest of the way back.

I left the plane and pilot at the dock. Didn't follow through on my first plan to burn the pilot with the Chief pilot. I just rescheduled with a different pilot the next day. I was worried about what John would say since the surveys weren't done. He was flying with Dick so I didn't find out until the next morning.

"Kim, did you forget Cholmondeley?" John asked after looking at my survey forms.

I'll never forget Cholmondeley. The first time I read a news release with Cholmondeley in it, I had pronounced it like its spelled Chol-mon- deley. "What?" the caller answered. Luckily, DeJong, the other assistant, was standing next to me and said "It's Chomlely" I felt like an idiot. "No, the pilot forgot to use both tanks and ran out of gas as we were crossing from Kasaan. We ended up with spruce branches in the floats before he figured out what he had done. I canceled the survey and I'm never flying with him again. I rescheduled with a different pilot today." I explained.

"Don't blame you. Be sure Michelle has the name so none of us fly with him. No excuse for running out of gas. Dick and I have had to search for a couple of bozos who ran out of gas but never a professional pilot."

Dick popped up on cue behind John and morning coffee turned into a discussion of running out of gas, bodies Dick had found on searches, and other related topics.

APPOINTMENTS IN THE BUSH

*Figure 17 Cessna 206H on amphibious
floats THABET AEROPLUS*

Don, Ketchikan Area Habitat Biologist, and I looked up and down the empty beach. I couldn't see a plane on the water or in the air. Looking at each other, then our watches, Don said "Guess we didn't need to put that rush on at the end.

They're late.

"Seems so. Not like Ketchikan Air, their usually right on time. Sorry I pushed." I walked up the beach a few steps to a drift log, shedding my daypack, I sat down. "Let's see what's left from lunch." Don joined me, pulling out the remains of the generous lunch Naomi had given him. "Guess I've been married to long. Marsha doesn't make my lunch anymore. Since she started doing tours with the bus company, she does bring home lots of goodies from the cruise ship lunches. I grab left-overs from the frig," I said.

"They feed those people pretty well, huh?" Don asked.

"Yeah, everyone going on the bus tours gets a big box lunch. With all the food on the ships, most people don't touch em. When Marsha cleans her bus, she ends up with five or ten of them, unopened. Fried chicken, pickles, tator chips, you name it. We have a well-stocked fridge. Handy stuff for lunches. Feel guilty about what gets thrown away but the tour company can't donate it because of some rule requiring inspection," I explained.

"Wow, you could bring some to the office," Don suggested.

"Hmm, that's a thought, not sure how folks would feel about throwaway lunches. Marsha gets to see where they've been."

Don was busy chewing. After swallowing he asked "How'd your hearing test go?."

"You didn't hear that story, huh. Another clue, I've been married too long. The audiologist called us both in and said, "Your hearing is perfect, honey." I'm not sure why women think it's OK to call customers, honey. But I digress. She said "There is a problem in a narrow range but most shooters we test show a loss there."

Marsha joined in asking, "But he doesn't hear anything I say and he keeps the TV and radio way too loud."

"Honey, how long have you been married?" She asked.

Marsha says, "Seven years."

Audiologist says, "Honey you got about two more years than most of us. It's selective hearing. All men get it. They don't hear their wives,."

"I didn't tell Marsha but I think women get it too," I added.

As Don laughed, I looked out across the sky over Carrol Inlet. I could see a tiny floatplane on the far shore. It landed at the mouth of a stream. "Rats."

"What?" Don said.

I pointed across the inlet, "Thought that might be our plane but it landed on the other side. Maybe they combined two charters. That'll save your budget a couple of bucks."

Don studied the far shore with his binoculars. "Looks like they're taking off."

I looked thru my binocs, sure enough the floats had the "bone in their teeth." Then it lifted off. It stayed low following the shoreline until it disappeared heading for the Carrol River. "Shit, that's disappointing. Better collect some dry wood so we can light signal fires if he comes back this way." (Three of anything is the international distress signal.

"Who are you kidding. There's nothing dry around here," Don said.

"That's what your handy dandy Swiss Army knife is for. We peel bark off the cedar trees. It doesn't burn long but if you have enough, it will get some of the other stuff dry enough to burn," I said.

"I guess it will give us something to do. When do we decide we're in survival mode?" Don asked.

I turned from the cedar tree I was assaulting. "Hell, when we started walking that road centerline, we entered survival mode. Our survival plan just got changed by the plane not showing up. I'm just passing time, it's coming. The signal fires are just in case we need to hitchhike home. Walking down the White River valley is one thing. Walking back uphill in the dark is beyond my job description. Anyway, I was born lazy."

Don gave a little snort, probably from the dusty bark he was striping rather than my attempt at humor. "You think we'll need to walk out?"

"It's an option. All the survival classes and books say to stay put, but that's if your lost," I said.

"Yeah, we aren't lost. Know right where we are. We're just abandoned or forgotten," Don said.

"Your right. Question is if we walk, would the hatchery be easier than walking back up that logging road right of way to the truck." I said.

"I think the hatchery is closer. I hear a plane!" Don said. We both headed back to our gear on the beach and grabbed our binoculars to begin searching north towards the engine sound. We found the plane. It was flying low along the shoreline, it appeared to be searching.

"Hamlin either got a new plane or he has competition for his beach logging," I said.

"Could be looking for us?" Don suggested.

"Nah, we haven't been missing long enough yet. Anyway, Ketchikan Air knows we're at the mouth of the White River," I said.

The plane made a course correction to follow the shoreline that put it mostly broadside in my binoculars. I was pretty sure I saw Ketchikan Air's paint scheme. "I think that's Ketchikan Air," I said.

"Why is he searching the shoreline?" Don asked.

"Beat's me. Maybe someone is missing and he's combining a search with our pick-up," I suggested.

"Wouldn't he do the charter first?" Don asked.

"Shit, you'd think so. Here he comes." The Ketchikan Air Cessna 206 swung in towards the mouth of the river and we made like little puppets, jumping up and down wildly waving our arms. The concern, we had carefully pent up, overrode our desire to behave like the experienced woodsmen we were, being released. Survival courses, scuba classes, flying school all had taught to stay clam no matter how scared you are. But sometimes you need a physical release.

The plane landed and taxied in, then shutdown and coasted in to the beach. The pilot jumped out, recognizing me said, "Finally found you. May have to fire our new dispatcher. She wrote down pick-up in Carrol Inlet. I've been flying the beach looking for you."

"We watched you," Don said.

Pointing to the pile of cedar bark, I added, "We were going to light fires but didn't have time."

"Good luck with that," The pilot said.

We helped turn the Cessna 206 around so it pointed out from the beach. The big six-seater was more plane than we needed but was still a welcome sight. The pilot held the plane while Don and I tossed our day packs behind the first row of rear seats, then Don took one. I buckled in the copilot's seat. On some previous flights our pilot, whose name I've forgotten, had checked me out flying the 206 but we hadn't done any takeoffs or landings. As he climbed in next to me, he said, "Don, is it alright if I let Kim do the takeoff?"

Poor Don what could he say but "Sure that's OK."

Great! Hope he really is all right with it. Here goes. Under the pilot's careful supervision, I started the plane. Took a short burst of power to free the floats from the beach. I dropped the rudders, there is a rudder at the end of each float, they are hinged so they can be raised to protect them when beaching the plane and taking off. They are used while taxing to steer the plane while it's a boat. I needed a little instruction on setting the constant speed prop to the takeoff position. My experience was all with fixed speed props on less complex planes.

The plane weathercocked into the wind, I raised the rudders, got a thumbs-up for remembering that, pushed the throttle to full, holding back on the yoke to keep the nose high and minimize the spray damage to the prop. The plane set back on its heels and began throwing a large white wake, known as the bone. As our speed increased the floats began rising on step, I relaxed pressure on the yoke letting the nose come down. We leveled off on the water, the airspeed indicator crossed the takeoff line, and I applied back pressure to the yoke. We lifted into the air. I climbed to around 1,500' and made a climbing turn to the south towards Ketchikan.

"Level out at 3,000, adjust the prop to cruise." Instructed the pilot.

This done, we cruised down Carrol Inlet, passed the new hatchery at the end of the road to Ketchikan. As we began passing the increasing number of houses that stretched along the road, the pilot said, "Nice job. We'll save landings for another day. I'll take it now."

The 206's floats were amphibious, as all Ketchikan Air's planes were so they were based at Ketchikan International Airport, located on Gravina Island, across Tongass Narrows from Ketchikan. (Many years later, the bridge built between Ketchikan and the airport would become famous as "The Bridge to Nowhere,). I paid close attention to the pilot's procedures as he brought the plane in for a landing on the relatively huge runway compared to the plane, we were in. He did a wheel landing, which, as we touched down, I realized was pretty much required by the amphibious floats. The wheels were so far below the pilot judging the flare height for a full stall landing would be tough. In addition, the wheels are smaller than on standard landing gear, plus they didn't look all that well sprung to me.

After tying down the plane we went into the office, Don wrote out the "Travel Authorization" so Ketchikan Air would receive payment for the trip. Checking this road alignment for minimal interference with a salmon stream was Habitat Division's responsibility. I was along as the "salmon expert" and for safety, plus a chance to get out of the office. The policy was not to be alone in the Alaskan wilderness. While Don was doing the paperwork, I called Marsha to ask her to pick us up at the ferry terminal.

"Well, we cheated death again." I said.

"It wasn't that bad." Don said. "It was a nice day on the beach. No rain, the centerline doesn't look like a problem. I think we did good." Don added.

"Yeah, that phrase is just my good luck charm. Marsha hates it. Don't know where I picked it up, but I say it after every flight and I'm still here." I explained.

We took seats on the bench in the waiting area at the ferry terminal.

"We just missed it. Now we're in for a long wait." Don observed as we watched the departing ferry.

"Yeah, we should have stopped for a beer at the lounge. Now we'll have to wait till we get home." Don and Naomi rented the upstairs apartment in our duplex, so we shared "home."

"That'll work. I'm tired and hungry. Wonder what's for supper." Don mused.

SAILBOATS AND BUZZING PLANES

Figure 18 Dick's PA-14 Francisco Photo

I was admiring a beautiful sailboat in full sail. That's what to do when I retire. Get a sailboat and sail around the world.

"Kim, do you have any idea how I could blow the wind out of that boat's sails with the propwash? I've been trying for years but never could get it to work." Dick shouted over his shoulder and the engine. I couldn't copilot with Dick, since his PA-14 only had a single seat and set of controls in the cockpit, passengers sat behind the pilot in a seat wide enough for two.

Thinking, I answered, "It's called dumping the wind, but sailing is just a dream of mine. No idea how you'd do it with the prop wash."

"OK, I've tried before. Didn't work. Try something new." Dick said as he adjusted the trim and commenced a power dive. Dick loved to buzz the boats of people he knew and some he didn't, so this wasn't a new maneuver for me. But as the masts approached closer and closer, I became concerned. This was a ketch rigged boat, main mast forward and a shorter mast stern. Suddenly, Dick pulled up to near vertical.

Must be trying to put the propwash down the inside of the sail. Might work.

TWANG, a shudder ran through the plane.

Shit, what did we hit, the floats! Are we going to be able to land!

"Shit, they're still sailing." Dick called.

Yep, sails still full. I got to ask. "*What did* we hit?"

"Don't know, don't see anything bent or broken, must have been the aerial on top of the mast. Look down out of the window and see if the floats look alright." Dick said.

I had already slid across the rear seat made for two in the PA-14 and was looking out the right side of the plane at the floats. Then slid back inspecting the left. *Don't see anything out of place here. Left side looks* good too.

"Dick, don't see any damage but there's a lot I can't see, under the plane." I announced.

"Yeah, have to land carefully." Dick replied.

Land carefully. How do you do that. Watch and learn.

We continued to salmon streams in Seaton Bay and Boca De Quadra. As we were crossing the roughest, highest mountain ridge between the two drainages, Dick reached down and grabbed an empty soda can from a bag at his feet. Opening the window, he let it go, fluttering down into the wilderness. Before I could accuse him of littering, he turned and faced me with a big grin.

"Now some mountain climber will struggle to get up where no one has ever been and find a pop can." Laughing he turned back to take us down to the Keta River, back to work.

That will be a big disappoint for someone. Not sure how I feel about littering the wilderness?

We were approaching Dick's floating hanger on the west side of Ketchikan after several hours of surveys, when I remembered the floats and the twang. Dick hadn't forgotten. He eased down to the water and a little nose high, he set the floats into the water but maintained flight speed. Nothing fell off. We settled into the water and taxied back to the hanger. He gently eased the bows of the floats onto the ramp, with a burst of power we slid up the ramp and into the hanger. Dick's PA-14 had been converted to a 150hp engine, earning it the name Super Cruiser. We climbed out and eagerly began inspecting the cross braces between the floats for signs of a strike. Sure enough, the front brace had a fresh scratch in the oxidized aluminum surface. No dents or sign of any other damage. Fingering the scratch Dick said, "Well that didn't dump the wind out of his sails. Have to try something different next time."

"I just hope he didn't get your number. Does anyone ever report you?" I asked.

"Not yet, guess they think I'm harmless." Dick replied.

My flights with Dick were always safe, fun, and educational. He had a huge wealth of local knowledge. I often wished that the PA-14 had dual controls so I could do a little of the flying but the seat arrangement didn't allow dual control. It seemed we often saw sailboats or recognized people we knew out fishing. These were always targeted for a buzz to break the routine of flying. Sadly, Dick never did dump the wind out of the sails of a boat while I was in Ketchikan. Here's hoping he finally succeeded.

SPENCER AIRCAR

Figure 19 S12D Air Car Mill Valley CA
Wikipedia Creative Commons

I **never forgot the fly-in at** Ottumwa, my first flight in the Ford Trimotor and all the wonderful homebuilt planes. As a result, I had joined the Experimental Aircraft Association reading the monthly publication from cover to cover and dreaming of building my own plane. (I subscribed to Small Boat Journal, too, and dreamed of building a boat. I do a lot of dreaming.) Over the years various entrepreneurs began advertising build-it-yourself kits. The magazine did articles on various kits covering equipment and ability requirements to complete the kits. Level of difficulty and flying characteristics of the completed aircraft. I dreamed of building my own plane but like my boat building dreams, they stayed dreams. Although I had built a kayak kit when I was about 14 that was a wonderful vessel that provided many hours of messing about on the water.

One day while I was stationed in Ketchikan, I was driving home with Marsha from Dick Hamlin's hangar. She had picked me up after a day of flying surveys counting salmon. As we approached the small public floatplane and amphibian plane docking area, I saw one of my dream homebuilt planes landing on Tongass Narrows. A Spencer Aircar, a 4-seat amphibious flying boat. I pulled over to watch quickly explaining to Marsha why and what we were watching. Her simple reply was "O Kim, really. It's just a plane." Her tone of voice spoke volumes.

The Aircar taxied off the narrows onto the public amphibian ramp. As it taxied up to the ramp, you could see the wheels coming out of the streamlining cover on the sides of the plane. As they reached the ramp, the pilot added power and the plane rolled up onto the ramp and into the small parking area.

"Their stopping, I've got to talk to them and get a closer look at the plane." I said.

Which was followed by a resigned "O Kim." From Marsha. That's not fair, she's usually the one starting conversations with strangers.

I pulled off the road and into the small parking area as the two occupants of the plane climbed out dry footed and began tying the plane down. I parked the Landcruiser nearby and jumped out, almost running over to them. "Hi, I'm Kim Francisco. That's a Spencer Aircar isn't it? Did you build it yourself?"

The pilot looked at me and extended his hand, which I took, saying "I don't usually receive such enthusiastic knowledgeable greetings in new towns. I'm (My apologies your names escape me so I'll make some up.) Paul Herring and this my partner Don Romper. Yes, we and the rest of the Boys Club built it in our hanger in San Francisco. The Boys Club is a group of guys who own and hangout in our spare time at our hanger. Come with me, I'll take you on a walkaround. Who's that waiting in the car?"

"My wife, Marsha. Is it OK for her to come on the walk around?"

"Sure."

I went back to the car and asked her if she wanted to walk-around the plane. "No, you boys have fun." But as I rejoined the pilot she did step out, unseen by me, I was all eyes and ears on the plane and my guide.

"This is officially a S-12-E since it has a Continental 285 horsepower engine. *That will be spendy, may not be for me.* It has a Hartzell reversible prop which is really handy for taxing on water. Capacity is four souls, we put dual controls in this one for teaching. Total length is 26 feet, wingspan 37'4." Cruise is 135 mph; range is 700 miles. We've really enjoyed our flight up the coast from San Francisco." As he was rattling off specs, we were walking around the plane and I was examining construction details.

"How long did it take to build?' How long would I have to rent part of Hamlin's hanger?"

"I'm not sure. All of us worked on it when we had time, didn't log our hours. We were about two years doing it. Different guys were good with the wood, fiberglass, or steel."

Done wood and fiberglass, steel! Probably need help. "Is there a lot of steel work?"

"No and it's just bending some tubes and a little welding. But most any welding shop would do it cheaply."

"Yeah but, big job for one person."

"That's for sure. If I didn't have the club, I would buy a Republic Seabee, that's the plane Spencer designed for Republic. When he left them, he designed this homebuilt version. You could fix-up a pretty beat-up Seabee for a lot less money and time."

"Thanks, something to think about." I answered. *One of those Seabees I've seen. Especially all polished and shiny would be nice. There's enough room Marsha might* be happy.

"Paul this phone doesn't work?" Don called from the payphone that was in small protective box on a pole.

I said "Our 18 feet of rain makes keeping outdoor electronics working tough. I can give you a ride to a phone or wherever?"

"That would be great, we have reservations at the hotel. Don was calling for a courtesy car."

As I began moving towards "Critter", Marsha's name for our Land Cruiser, Don and Paul retrieved overnight bags from the plane, locking the doors behind them. Marsha was standing next to Critter and I said "We're going to drop them at the hotel before we go home."

"OK, would they like supper, just chili tonight." She answered as she opened the passenger door, folded down the seat and climbed into the back.

"Don't do that we can ride in the back?" Don said to her.

"It's more comfortable for me, my legs are shorter. Put your bags back here with me." Marsha instructed.

"Your awfully kind to strangers." Paul said.

"Hey, we pilots all need a ride now and then." I said as we packed into Critter's 40-60 front seat.

Paul and Don began talking to Marsha about her job driving a tour bus for the cruise ship passengers. They passed on supper so I dropped them at the hotel downtown where they had reservations. The next day was Saturday so I offered to pick them up in the morning if they needed a ride or a tour. Paul and Don declined "We can get a cab."

"No, I much rather give you a ride." I insisted

"OK, but two conditions, we buy you two breakfast and let you fly the plane."

"Hey that would be great. What time?"

"About eight would be fine. Where should we have breakfast?"

"Don't usually eat out for breakfast but the fishermen I work with tell me the Marine Café is the place to eat."

"OK, then we'll see you both at eight."

Next morning, we picked Paul and Don up at the hotel for the short trip to the Marine Cafe. We three guys talked planes and homebuilding them. Marsha was a little bored with not much to say. As was her way, she struck-up a conversation with the waitress, a complete stranger. As it turned out, the waitress, was a fascinating woman who we all began questioning. She was in her fifties, had decided after graduating from high school to see the world. Seemed like there were jobs for waitresses everywhere so she became the best waitress she could, as a result the conversation was often interrupted as she spotted an empty coffee cup, took or delivered an order. She told us she strayed till she tired of a place then moved on. Ketchikan was her last stop in Alaska, then she was headed to Hawaii to finish the fifty states.

"Fascinating way to live your life." Commented Paul as he covered the bill with enough money for breakfast and a generous tip. "Let's go flying."

Paul was briefing me on takeoff and stall speeds along with other important information on flying the Aircar. Don and Marsha buckled safety into the passenger seats, Paul took the pilot's seat and I settled into the copilot spot. Paul took me through a very complete instrument panel. While paying attention to where everything was, I was also trying to run a tally of cost based on adds in EAA magazine. Lost count. It's a lot.

Pay attention. One of my life long challenges was my mind was always wondering and or wandering.

Paul fired up the big 285 hp Continental Tiara. With the pusher engine setup, the sound was surprising quiet in the cabin. I suppose because the engine and prop were behind instead of in front of the cabin but that big engine was still impressive. My Taylorcraft and Luscombe had both been powered with Continental 85 horse.

By depressing the tops of the rudder pedals with his feet, a common toe-brake mechanism, Paul taxied to the top of the ramp. Turning down the ramp we nosed into the water. He taxied out of the little harbor and into Tongass Narrows. In the process I cranked-up the wheels. Out in the channel Paul pointed out the takeoff check list and said, "Take her up." I let the plane weathercock into the wind while calling the tower requesting takeoff instructions. They asked me to stand by so we continued taxing basically motionless since the engine on idle overcame the wind and current. The tower called "S12E cleared for takeoff." I did a quick final checklist check, gear up and locked, seatbelts, everyone was buckled, checked the water and sky ahead for traffic, and added throttle.

"She can take it faster." Paul instructed. I pushed the throttle in faster. The nose lifted blocking the forward view and water spray blocked the view to the sides. *This low to the water want to be sure takeoff path is clear.* Then she climbed onto step and the nose dropped as we accelerated and I could see again. The spray was gone now as we raced down the Narrows. The airspeed indicator reached the green line that marked flight speed I pulled back on the yoke and we lifted gently into the air. I dropped the nose immediately after takeoff to gain airspeed. I noticed the lag Paul had warned me of, pusher aircraft such as the Aircar, respond slower than tractor aircraft to throttle and attitude changes.

Slower probably not really the right word, but it's the one everyone uses. The feel is different. Actually, smoother might be more accurate than slower.

I flew us up the Narrows, the short distance to Mountain Point made a turn over George Inlet and headed back towards Ketchikan.

"We need to get gas at Weber Air, can you take us there?" Paul asked.

"Sure, I better give it back to you for the landing."

"No, you can do it."

Glad you think so. It does fly nice. Maybe I can do it. Call the tower dummy. I called the tower and they cleared us to land at Weber Air. I flew around Pennock Island as my downwind leg, used the base leg to get back to the Ketchikan side and landed upwind. My caution resulted in a long base leg so I landed a little past Weber. *Shit, still a pretty good landing with a strange plane. I didn't bounce.* "Paul, you better take it in to the dock, Weber is just behind us."

"Nice job for your first time." Paul said taking the controls.

"Yes, you need one of these." Don added.

Paul taxied us in very gently pulling into the dock where a line boy tied us up. I checked on Marsha who was prone to airsickness. She was OK and didn't want to wait at Weber's until I came back with the car. Plane refueled, everyone back in the line-boy said, "I'll turn you around."

"No need." Paul answered. "Clear!" He started the engine. "Watch this." He said. As the plane began backing away from the dock, the line-boy was calling everyone out to see a plane backing up. "This reversable prop gets them every time. Even in B.C., where they've seen a lot of twin Otters on floats that can reverse, they hadn't seen a piston engine that could."

Paul made the short hop back to the dock at the amphibian ramp. Don, Paul, Marsha and I said our goodbyes and thank yous. Then Paul and Ben took off to the North to see Alaska.

"Marsha, I need to build one of those."

"We'll see."

FIELD BIOLOGIST
AND TOURISTS

Figure 20 Wien Air Alaska Boeing 737
courtesy of Al Ingle Capital Avionics

Joe was charging at full throttle across Kotzebue Sound. I turned my back to the bow, taking a firm steadying grip on the boat-seat, hunkering down with my head almost between my knees. My concern for a broken coccyx almost driving the terrible speculations about why Ron had called for my immediate return to Anchorage. Had Marsha been in a car accident? Attacked? Maybe it was Dad? His drinking and driving finally catching up to him. Or a heart attack? The house burned down? Why hadn't he told Joe what the problem was? Federal fiscal year was over next month, maybe the ANILCA (Alaska National Interest Lands Conservation Act) jobs were being cut. And I was out of a job? What was it?

My trip had started interestingly enough. Joe had taken me back out to the airport after I had spent a couple of days doing some Alaska National Interest Land Claims Act work with the US National Park Service in Kotzebue. They were clueless about their new parks and wild and scenic rivers they were now in charge of. Guess that's why they funded the state coordinator positions like mine.

Joe, Assistant Arctic Area biologist, was a great guy but with some interesting habits. He bought new pair of Carhart bib overalls at the beginning of every summer. Then wore them every day till the end of the season without washing them. He said he threw them away, but Claudia Regnart, Ron's wife, was sure they just ran away. He admitted by late August hardened fish slime and blood usually made it possible for them to stand in a corner by themselves. So maybe they could run or at least walk away at the end of the season.

Luckily for me, unlike most Regions, A-Y-K (Arctic, Yukon, Kuskokwim) didn't have a Regional Management Coordinator. Someone who supervised the management biologists and assisted as needed if job demands, illness, or sadly, sometimes death would interfere with their serving the public. Ron had started using me to handle some of the trouble shooting and assisting tasks he didn't have time for, that normally would be handled by a coordinator. He and the Regional Research Supervisor had noticed some friction between Joe and Doug (I apologize to the actual person I cannot remember your name.) the research biologist stationed in Kotzebue. I had been given the unenviable task of trying to find and solve the problem. It was "lucky" for me because it meant I was being trusted, trained, or tested, maybe all three for the requested but still nonexistent Regional Management Coordinator's position. Which would be a nice promotion and new job when the funding for ANILCA coordinators positions dried up.

Enough alphabet soup, my coordination with the Feds done in Kotzebue, Joe took me back to the airport, where he introduced me to a bush pilot, Johnny Walker. I smiled during our introduction and Johnny told me his father had owned the liquor store before Kotzebue went dry. He had named his two sons Johnny and Hiram, in honor of a couple of his biggest sellers.

We loaded my gear and the rest of the Department's gear that hadn't made the first flight with Doug, into the Supercub. I climbed into the rear passenger seat; Johnny got in in front of me. Supercub's, more properly PA-18, have tandem seating, that is the passenger sits behind the pilot. Only one passenger can go at a time, which is why I was following Doug in on a second flight. Johnny was an excellent pilot, using his checklist during the engine runup and taking off smoothly. We cruised over the Noatak River valley, flying high enough that we could follow a straight line to the gravel bar where he had dropped Doug and the inflatable boat. The hills surrounding the Noatak were beautiful. The tundra was changing into its fall colors, mostly yellows and reds. It was August but winter comes early above the Arctic Circle.

The landing was smooth and gentle. The big soft "Tundra" tires absorbing a lot of the roughness usually felt in gravel bar landings. The three of us quickly unloaded the plane and Johnny taxied to the downwind end of the bar, turning around and making a picture perfect takeoff.

Doug and I assembled the rowing frame, inflated the boat and attached the frame. Then we launched the boat, anchoring it to shore in shallow water. Then we loaded the gear, tent, sleeping bags, and dehydrated food for two weeks. Our only possible connection to help the emergency locator beacon I kept safely rolled up in my sleeping bag. We had lunch, then rowed out into the river, making a short trip to the next gravel bar, where we landed. Arming ourselves with our sampling gear, we headed down the bar, examining each dead chum salmon for tags and also collecting the sex, length, and a scale from the carcasses, tagged and untagged. We stopped at every pool carefully looking at the salmon swimming there. If one was wearing a Petersen disk tag, an orange plastic nickel sized disk, we used our frog gig spear to collect the fish and recover the tag. Often salmon who had died after spawning weren't washed up on the gravel bar but lay at the bottom of the pools, usually covered in a white fungus. If an orange tag was showing we speared up these fish too for tag recovery. My nose quickly became "blind" to the smell.

Doug and his tagging crew had tagged the salmon in Kotzebue Sound. He was now recovering the tags from the Kobuk and Noatak Rivers. These are the two primary tributaries and spawning streams flowing into the Sound. This would provide a great deal of information, population size, run timing, migration speed, and such that would assist in managing the fishery.

It was an interesting two weeks, in addition to the salmon, we often saw river otters, beavers, and caribou. Bird watching was great and the arctic char fishing was so good it became boring. Occasionally, a brown bear or bear family we're picnicking on a prospective bar. Despite the seven shot riot gun we carried, loaded with alternating slugs and buckshot, we left them undisturbed. We wondered how many tags ended up in bear scat.

As we approached the mouth of the Noatak, it slowed down and got wider. Salmon became harder to find. Triangulating off some prominent landmarks one morning, Doug and I determined we were not drifting downstream but the headwind was carrying us upstream. Doug said, "Joe was supposed to start checking for us yesterday. We're close enough, he should find us soon. Let's break out the outboard."

Doug had planned for this eventually by bringing along a one and a half horsepower outboard that had been resting quietly on the motor mount hung over the stern tube. I dug down through the gear to a five gallon can of premixed gas. Properly fed, the little outboard popped to life, the tiny single cylinder motor sounding more like a toy than a motor. It had the desired effect and we once again continued very slowly downstream. Looking for Joe, who didn't find us until shortly after we started the next morning.

Doug began to harangue him about being late. Joe cut him short. "Ron, called and want's Kim in Anchorage ASAP. Kim get your gear. I think I can get you on Alaska Air's next flight. Doug, I'll come back for you."

As I loaded my gear and self into the skiff, I asked "Did Ron say what the rush was for?"

"Nope. Hang on." Joe hit the throttle but my mind raced faster than the boat.

The Kotzebue Airport is located right along the beach. The water is deep right up to the gravel fill for the runway. I expect that DOT had mined gravel from the Sound's bottom for construction. Joe nosed in to the steep gravel bank. I was already wearing my pack carrying my briefcase. Climbing out I said "Thanks Joe, think I've got it from here.", over my shoulder since I was struggling with the shifting gravel footing on the steep bank.

"Hope everything turns out to be OK." Joe called as he backed away, turning to return for Doug.

At my best speed, I jogged across the runway to the terminal, rushed through the doors up to the Alaska Air Lines desk. Breathing heavily, I hadn't run so far since high school. I gasped out "Hi Kim Francisco, gasp, I have a reservation, gasp, on the next flight, gasp, to Anchorage." Between gasps I was unzipping and digging out my open return ticket out of the front pocket of my REI briefcase. I handed the ticket to the agent as she answered.

"We'll have to hurry, it's boarding now." She tore out a ticket, whacking everything with her hand stamp. "Do you have any luggage to check?"

"Err, yep." I began struggling with my pack. Some unknown, unseen person behind me came to my rescue, lifting the pack so I could shrug it off my shoulders. I turned to thank them as I grabbed the pack to put it on the scale but no one was there. I heard the stapler and turned back to the agent who handed me my boarding pass and pointing, she said "That gate."

"Thank you." I said as I raced for a door where an agent was just announcing the last call for my flight. I flashed her my boarding pass and rushed out the door onto the runway. Ran to the moveable stairway at the back of a blue and yellow Wein Air 737. A stewardess was waiting at the top of the stairs, gasping I handed her my ticket and boarding pass.

"You're the last one. It's open seating." She said, handing the ticket back. Her nose wrinkling.

Cute smile. "Thanks" I gasped stepping inside as she pulled the door shut behind me.

As I looked for a seat, it was obvious that this was primarily an Arctic Circle tourist flight. All the airlines run them out of Anchorage, for a special rate, they get to cross the Arctic Circle and visit Kotzebue; an Alaskan native village. There's a salmon lunch and the local Inupiat dancers put on a show of traditional dancing. It's a small but very incomplete taste of village life. I knew these people were tourists by looking since they were all neat and clean, dressed like city slickers on the weekend. The few Alaskans on board, men and women, were in uniform, like me, work pants, flannel or wool shirt and a baseball cap. The difference was they were clean and they were wearing their best clean Alaskan uniform. I became a little self-conscious of the clothes I had been wearing for two weeks. The fact my underwear was clean was a great comfort to me but didn't show. I had learned that a fresh t-shirt and shorts felt almost as good as a shower out in the field. I always carried enough for the expected stay.

Fortunately for me, there was a window seat open in the front row, facing the door that let the crew pass through the sliding wall into the cargo area and on to the cockpit. I always preferred that row if I could get it because of the leg room. Some people were put off by the lack of a tray table. The seat in front of the inside passage way door was avoided because of the traffic or sometimes it was reserved by the stewardess. I walked through the cabin, the chatter stopping. I barely noticed, my mind returning to speculation of why I had been recalled. I nodded and said "Good afternoon." To the two people in the aisle and center seat, next to my empty window seat. They gave me an unpleasant look. *Impolite jerks, they could at least* say hi.

I sat taking my book out of my briefcase, sliding the case under my seat, buckled my seat belt and tried to blot out my thoughts with reading. Didn't work.

The stewardess suddenly arrived and leaned down to whisper with the couple next to me. I couldn't hear what was said. Standing and scanning the passengers, she took the arm of the lady next to me and led the pair off down the aisle. I tried to concentrate on my book. The stewardess returned and did her preflight safety talk. I always listen and follow along even though I know the 737's safety talk by heart. People forget the real reason for stewardesses and stewards is their safety. Shit happens, albeit rarely but you deal with it better if your prepared. As she returned to the back of the plane, I was counting the rows to the nearest exit. In an emergency, the lights go first and if the dark isn't bad enough smoke further blinds you. My mother's blind cousin had taught me you should know the way out of anywhere by feel.

The guy on the aisle in the row behind mine, stopped her, whispering something to her. She assured him she'd take care of it after takeoff, which started while she was still taking her seat. After takeoff, I was still wondering why I was returning early, trying to concentrate on the book instead, with no success, worrying about my wife and family. When I remembered Ron had told me Doug and Joe had not been getting along. Since I was going to be in Kotzebue, he had asked me to see if I could get to the bottom of it and offer a solution. I had pretty well covered Doug's side during our two weeks of campfire chats and had heard Joe's side while I spent a couple days bunking in with him before recovering tags. Interpersonal relationships were not my thing but it was a relief to be off wondering about Marsha. The Francisco curse, people brought their problems to my Dad and I had found the same thing was happening to me. People were usually pleased with my advice; I don't know why. I didn't think there was much to do about Doug and Joe. They just were different types and would probably never be good friends but they were professional enough to still work together. I wasn't sure that would satisfy Ron and Bill but it was all I had.

The plane leveled off at cruise altitude. The stewardess rearranged the people in the row behind me, opening up three seats. Then she escorted the people in the second row behind me to seats further back. I assumed that people wanted to sit with friends or family hadn't been able to choose the desired seats when boarding. Back to my book and worries. I was vaguely, aware that seat shuffling was still going on which was a little unusual, but I had problems.

"Hi Kim, guess I'll be joining you. No one else wants to sit with a biologist fresh out of the field." I looked up, and I mean up. My new seat mate was a very tall man, with a full beard, who was a research biologist with Game Division, we had been acquainted since college.

Surprised at this new information and the interruption of my dark thoughts I was brilliant, answering "What?"

"You stink. These poor touristas (A word invented by Alaskans to disparage the state's second largest source of income.) aren't use to the smell of rotten salmon. They all asked the stew to be moved away from you. Guess I must have looked like a biologist so she asked me if I would sit next to you. She was running out of seats in the back." Alex said. (Another name I had to make up.)

I looked around and saw lots of empty seats and the passengers all packed into the rows furthest away from me. "Wow, that bad huh."

"It's nothing, these people should get a whiff of a rotting whale." He said.

"Yeah, whales are the worst. Wonder if it's the size or composition or both."

"Don't know how the flies stand it. Don't think there's anything worse than rotten whale. The rendering plant in Des Moines came close. Maybe smell increases logarithmically with volume." I added.

He laughed, "I see why Tina (His main squeeze and a friend of mine.) enjoys talking to you. What was that one liner you killed the ornithology class with?"

The plane made a sudden short climb followed by a sudden descent, causing some gasps among the passengers. "Ladies and gentlemen, we just crossed the Arctic Circle." The pilot announced.

"Guess they do that both ways. Regulars must get a little tired of it." I continued "Yeah, Dave, Dr. Norton, caught me talking to Tina during the lecture and asked "Kim, what is the family name of woodpeckers?" "Dildoformes" I popped off. Thought Dave was going to burst suppressing his laughter." (All the bird families in scientific nomenclature end in "formes", dildo is self-explanatory). But Dildoformes isn't the correct name, a play on the word woodpecker.

"Yes! That's it. Tina said about half the class, always expecting you to have the right answer, wrote it in their notes. A quarter looked puzzled and the rest laughed. How'd you come up with that on the spur of the moment?" Alex asked.

"Wish I could claim comedic talent but my roommate had been drilling me on bird families a night or two before. I was getting bored and so started screwing around making up better names. That was the only one that actually worked. Do sometimes wish I had taken Latin instead of Spanish and German." I replied.

"Good thing you didn't. It doesn't help at all. Scientific names are Latinized versions of so many other languages, real Latin doesn't help much." Alex commented.

I explained about my "emergency recall" being the reason for my filthy condition and thanked him for being willing to sit with me. We chatted the rest of the way to Anchorage. Ron and Tina were waiting at the gate when we disembarked so we went our separate ways. I said "Hi" to Tina from a distance, didn't want to expose her to the smell and I wanted to talk to Ron.

"Hi Ron, what's up?" I tried to say casually.

"Kim, I'm not sure how serious this is." He said fatherly. "I got a call from the troopers two days ago. They found Marsha asleep in her car by the side of the road, up by Palmer. She drove home but they were concerned with her behavior and we're trying to reach you as part of a welfare check. Claudia and I went out to visit and she says she's alright but she's running at 100 mph. I called Joe to get you back ASPA. You're going to have to get her to a doctor. Claudia and I would have taken her but she thinks she's fine."

Trying to take it all in, I said "OK and thank you. Thank Claudia too. I got Doug's and Joe's stories but didn't settle anything. That issue is still unresolved."

"Forget that. Taking care of Marsha is your priority now." He told me.

"Yeah, I'm just clearing the decks in my mind. Not sure what this could be. She has been losing a lot of weight. If she's using speed, she hiding it well." I said as we reached the luggage claim where my pack was already going around in circles.

"Speed! You don't think it's that?" Ron said as I snagged my pack.

"No, she's always been really down on drugs even the ones the Doc gives her. But she did think she was fat and so was trying to lose. Was really proud of the weight she was losing. But I can't imagine she was on diet pills. I'm just having trouble thinking of a cause." I said.

"You're a fish bio, not a Doc. Don't try to diagnosis. Lose weight, where did she get an idea like that. She wasn't even plump." Ron's seriousness changed to a light-hearted tone, which was reassuring.

"Probably shouldn't call her for a ride, huh?" I asked.

"No, if your car isn't here, I'll give you a lift."

"It's way out of your way. You've done enough already. Let me call a cab." I replied.

"Nope, this way, you're coming with me." Ron said leading the way to his familiar station wagon, which brought back memories of sleeping in the back while we were steelhead fishing. After exchanging some fish stories, I told Ron about driving the passengers away on the plane. He laughed but said "You're not bad. I've smelled a lot worst." Which lead us into a new topic of bad smells as he made the half hour drive to my house in Chugiak.

Marsha turned out to be hyperthyroid. Serious but treatable so my scariest flight turned out alright. My apologies to my fellow passengers.

HERRING

Figure 21 Cessna 185 Mark Pilkingtonwww.skywagons.com

"**I'm, Dee Jonrow, the Kuskokwim** Area Biologist, added herring biomass surveys at Nelson Island to the herring operational plan but never had the budget or time to get them done." They are so dependent on subsistence herring out there that we've pretty much ignored it since there was no interest in a commercial harvest. We've kept the foreign fleet out by telling them at the negotiations the herring were fully utilized by the Islanders. But now they want to know the biomass and the subsistence harvest. So, they can see if they are fully utilized. Mary Pete, with Subsistence Division, is doing the subsistence harvest survey but we need to get the biomass estimate. We also need some samples for age structure and such. You need to learn how to do aerial herring biomass since we don't do the hydroacoustic surveys like you did in Southeast. So, you and I are flying out to Bethel to do the survey and pick up a sample for Craig's herring crew. Tomorrow weather is supposed to be good. The Hooper brothers are supposed to collect the sample. Should be a simple job." Ron told me.

"Great! I'm getting a little tired of commenting on the ANILCA drafts." I replied.

"Good, meet me at Alaska Air at seven tomorrow morning."

"OK." Ron turned and headed down the hall back to his office. I marked my place in the environmental assessment I was reviewing and looked up at the clock. It was about two in the afternoon; my usual day was 7:00A.M. to 3:30 P.M. Didn't have to dodge so many Glen Highway road warriors on my way to and from work that way. Marsha and I lived in Chugiak, an Anchorage suburb that was about 30 miles from the ADF&G office. Since I had to get ready for the trip, I was going to knock-off a little early. Not really, since I would spend more than the hour and a half getting ready. I also had to check with Craig Whitmore, Herring Project leader, since he and I car pooled together.

First, I pulled my herring survey package and operational plan out of my file and put in my briefcase. I would review the plan that evening. I added the herring tube, inclinometer and tape recorder to the briefcase. I picked-up the clip board and headed down the hall to the herring office. Craig and the rest of the gang were all out in the field but the Xeroxes of the Nelson Island navigational charts were easy to find. Then I slipped out the side door, next to Craig's office, into the parking lot. *Rae advised me to never let them promote me above FBII and get a research job with an office next to the back door. He'd be ashamed if he saw me now. FBIII stuck in meetings and paperwork. A day in the field tomorrow will be great. Teaching me how to survey herring means Ron has some field work in mind for my future. At least my office is close to the side door.* This and additional pleasant thoughts occupied my mind as I drove up a relatively deserted Glen Highway with National Public Radio for company. Rush hour would start soon.

Marsha dropped me at the Alaska Air terminal the next morning. I met Ron at the gate and we had an uneventful 737 flight to Bethel. Our pilot was an old hand and new about the Bethel Bump in the runway so set down long to miss it. Poor DOTPF (Department of Transportation and Public Facilities) had been trying for years to find a paving technique that kept that patch of permafrost from heaving the runway without success.

Doug Bue, between crew leader jobs in the field, met our flight with "Tunes." An orange Ford F100 with Fish& Game stickers on the doors covering the old DOTPF stickers. For some reason, it had come with a radio. Most state vehicles didn't, the added cost of an "entertainment package" being a luxury state employee didn't deserve, according to the Administration. There were only two stations to choose from in Bethel. A "born again" station run by a local church and KYUK, the public radio station run by the Bethel Community College, part of the University of Alaska. It was run by volunteers and had programing in both Yup'ik and English. The music was mainly current Pop so it was the preferred station by most of the seasonals.

Tunes other unique accessory was a pair of vice grip pliers locked on a tiny stub of the ignition key. Rae Baxter, the Kuskokwim Area Research biologist, hated looking for keys. So, on Tunes fist day as an ADF&G truck he had broken the key off in the ignition. Clamped on the vice grip and presto, you could start Tunes whenever you wanted.

Doug dropped us at Hagland's Air, a 200-yard ride, where we climbed into a Cessna 185 and headed for Nelson Island. We started our survey at the village of Toksook Bay. Almost immediately we saw a huge dark mass with the occasional strobe like flash of sunlight reflecting off herring which had turned sideways towards the surface. I had seen this before in southeast Alaska while mapping herring spawn.

Ron said "Wow. This is huge. Start the stop watch. Measure the width." I started the stop watch and began taking measurements of the school's width with the little piece of plastic plumbing pipe with a scale, Xeroxed onto clear plastic transparency paper glued in place in a pair of slits cut into the tube. The nine-inch tube of plastic pipe didn't look like much but a lot of geometry had gone into calculating the grid and length so you could get the base of a triangle from it. Altitude of the plane gave you the triangle's height. On small schools you might also measure the length and width to calculate the area. The tube couldn't measure the length of a school this big, so with the speed of the plane and length of time it took to fly it, we calculated the length. W would measure the width at various landmarks on the map, then use a planimeter to measure the area of our drawing on the copy of the map. Ron and I were quiet, busy taking width measurements and keeping the location of the measurements on the map on our clip boards. The school began narrowing and finally petered out just before we reached Cape Vancouver.

Lifting his head and turning in his seat to face me, Ron said "That's the biggest school I've seen in A-Y-K. That's going to throw a kink in the negotiations.

"I think that's the biggest school I've ever seen. Their starting again." I said as I raised my tube to my eye. The pilot had been following the shoreline around Cape Vancouver but almost as soon as we rounded the point another herring school began. Thick and dark, it continued past the village of Tununak, finally petering out in the mud flats around Kigigak Island. "Wow. That was exciting!" I said as I raised my head.

"Yeah. That was something." Ron replied. As the pilot asked "Keep following the coast?"

"No, we need to land in Tununak and pick-up a herring sample." Ron replied. The pilot turned back to Tununak, where he made a routine landing and parking the plane in the small parking area near a tiny warm-up shack at the end of the runway.

"Gee, someone usually meets planes." The pilot commented.

"Yeah. Must not be expecting a mail plane." Ron said.

"Guess we have to walk. Let's head to the store. I need a Coke. The plane will be alright. Let's go," the pilot said. The three of us headed off down the road to the village.

No one seemed to be about as we walked through town and arrived at the store. As I started up the stairs, I almost fell when I tripped on the steps. Ron chuckled saying "The stairs aren't standard height here. There're lower to accommodate the Hoopers."

Regaining my footing and watching where I put my feet, I discovered the stairs were about half the normal height and took some thought to use since you had to overcome the muscle memory in your legs. "Why are they like this?"

"The Hooper brothers have Tununak Syndrome. Their legs are paralyzed below the knee so they have to walk on their knees." The pilot explained.

As we walked through the store, I said "That's really nice of the village to accommodate them. All the stairways in town like that? What's Tununak Syndrome?"

"Yes, all the stairways at public places, not sure about all the stairways to houses. Hang on. Could you give me directions to the Hooper House?" Ron asked the man behind the store's counter.

As the counterman gave us directions, the pilot arrived with his can of soda. "I'll meet you guys back at the plane. He said as he completed his transaction.

Ron said "Let's head for the Hoopers." As we walked out, he explained. "Tununak Syndrome was the name a doctor gave to what crippled the Hoopers. No one knows if its genetic or a disease.5"

We walked the short distance to the Hooper house and knocked on the door. There was no answer. "Great. Bill said they would be waiting for us. You wait here. I'm going to ask around and see if I can find them." Ron instructed.

"OK. I should have brought a book."

"Yea, just like the Army. Hurry up and wait." Ron said as he turned to go. He was stopped by the noisy arrival of Honda Three-wheeler. An average looking Yup'ik man pulled up and introduced himself as we did with handshakes all around. He was one of the Hoopers (I'm sorry I've forgotten which.).

"Hi. I come from herring pit." He explained.

"O, Bill just told us you had the herring didn't explain where to meet you." Ron explained.

"OK, tea? get herring?" Mr. Hooper asked.

"Thank you for offering but I think we should have tea another time. Let's get the herring." Ron replied.

"Follow me." Mr. Hooper left slowly on the three-wheeler. We followed him to a stretch of tundra just above the high tide line. There was a line of pieces of plywood weighed down with rocks stretching out in the beach grass just behind the high tide line. Mr. Hooper stopped at one. "Morning herring here." He dismounted and I noticed for the first time that the sealskin boots I had been admiring were actually sown into the knees of his heavy wool pants. His knees rested on the boot soles. He seemed very mobile walking right around to the seaward end of the plywood. He was

---

5   While living in Bethel a few years latter a team of doctors looking into "Tununak Syndrome" determined it was actually miss-diagnosed polio.

just shorter than most. His shins and feet were enclosed in fabric sticking out of the back of the boots. The cuffs were sewn shut. *I'd really like a picture but probably people are always asking him for pictures. I better* not ask.

I bent and grabbed the shoreside of the plywood to help him lift it off. Underneath was a pit dug into the tundra full of fresh herring. Mr. Hooper explained "We store herring couple of days. Easier split. Just thumb, no knife." Just behind us were driftwood racks holding ropes of drying herring. They had been gutted, opened up like a book. The herring's "neck", the narrow spot behind the head and gills was woven into the grass rope, then spread apart. The body was then open to the air as each fish hung from the rope. I couldn't imagine the amount of work involved.

"Caught morning tide." Mr. Hooper said.

"These will be perfect." Ron replied.

"You sample now?"

"No, Kim here is going to put two hundred in plastic bags. We'll sample them back in Bethel. There's a sampling crew there."

While Ron and Mr. Hooper talked about sampling and fishing. That's why the village seemed empty. Most of the men were out fishing. The women were resting from processing yesterday's herring. I got out the box of "Steel Sacks" I was carrying in my brief case. This was currently the thickest "garbage bag" available off the shelf. Quite popular for honey buckets and in our case, herring samples, anything where spillage was unpleasant and unwanted. There was a plastic bucket turned over with a rock on top of the bottom to keep it from blowing away nearby. Waiting for an opening in the conversation, I asked Mr. Hooper "Is it OK if I use the bucket as a herring scoop?"

"OK. That way we use."

I set the rock aside and picked-up the bucket and pushed it into the herring. They were still wet and slippery so just like lumpy water. It took no effort to slide the bucket in, turn it upright, and it was full of herring. I had taken a belt and suspenders approach, putting one steel sack inside the another. Opening the doubled sack, I put it over the bucket. I then grabbed the bucket with the sacks and turned it over. The herring poured into the empty flaccid sack giving it a little shape. I repeated the process but just used the empty top of the sacks over the bucket. Watching, Ron said "You've done this before?"

"Many times, back in southeast. We often transferred herring samples from buckets to sacks. The Sundance's skipper didn't like slimy herring buckets on his boat. I'm running out of empty sack. These Nelson Island herring are bigger than I'm used to. Could you hold it open while I pour in the next bucketful?

"Sure, I don't get a chance to get close to fish anymore. Always in some damn meeting."

I poured in another bucketful. "I think that fills the sack." I turned to set the bucket down. Ron let go of the top of the sack to get the data sheet with location, date, and mesh size out of his notebook to put into the sack. Instead of sitting open, the herring flowed to the low side of the sack and began spilling out. As herring flowed onto the ground, I dropped the bucket, fell to my knees, grabbed the top of the bag pulling it up. Stopping the flow of fish. Looking up, I saw Ron on his knees busy collecting the 10 or 15 herring that had "escaped" onto the ground. They were so big he could only hold a couple at a time but he quickly gathered them up and dropped them into the bag. Followed by the data sheet. Grinning at me, he said "Now you're my witness. I still get fish slime on my hands. Nobody's going to believe you got me to handle herring."

"I'm sorry.

"Don't be, it's great to be a fisheries biologist again." Ron answered.

I double knotted the top of the bag and started on the second bagful. Mr. Hooper kindly offered to take them to the plane with the little trailer he had for his three-wheeler. Ron and I walked behind, talking about our recent steelhead fishing trip down on the Kenai Peninsula. We loaded the herring in next to my seat in the plane. The pilot had removed the right passenger seat since only three of us were flying. We waved goodbye to the departing Mr. Hooper. As we climbed into the plane I said "You know three-wheelers have this bad reputation for crippling people. Here they have given mobility to two paralyzed men. It's all about context."

"Yeah. We still really get good use out of them even if that accident on the Yukon cost the state some money."

"Hey, that guy thought it was great. Got all his medical paid and got his salary until December instead of getting laid off at the end of August. He couldn't believe it."

"How did that work?" The pilot asked.

"Workmen's Comp. Insisted he be paid until he was fit to return to work, even though there wasn't any work. Didn't seem quite right, but I guess if he had been crippled for life, it might have been. Not sure how you make this stuff fit all situations." Ron replied.

"All strapped in. Clear." The pilot shouted out the window and started the engine. After a short warm-up, we taxied out onto the runway headed in to the wind. The pilot announced our take-off intention on the airport's radio frequency. No response so he hit the power and we started down the runway, gravel flying. He smoothly lifted the tail, as we gained speed then smoothly lifted the nose and plane into the air. As the plane's pitch, increased the bags of herring began to flow back into the plane's fuselage. I saw it out of the corner of my eye and made a grab. I got a knot in my right hand but I just barely got a corner of the second bag with my left as it slipped into the cone leading to the tail.

"What's happening back there? I'm losing control." The pilot shouted as he pushed the yoke and throttle forward to fight the rising pitch of the nose caused by the weight of the herring and me moving aft. I unfastened my seatbelt. *What if we crash? If the herring slip into the tail we will crash.*

Shit. Free of the seat, I turned leaning over the bag of herring, which of course, shifted more weight aft of the center of gravity, worsening the pitch.

I hollered "The herring are sliding into the tail! I'm trying!" The main mass of herring was in the bag stretching it to what I feared was the breaking point. As I rose on my knees to try and get a hold that would let me pull the bag back forward. I once again shifted the center of gravity aft. The pilot swore as he tried to keep control. The situation worsened or improved as Ron released his seat belt and leaned back grabbing my belt. This allowed me to lean out to get my knee on the floor so the bag of herring in my right hand was trapped against my thigh. Both hands free, I began grabbing the flowing bag hand over hand. The bag kept flowing away from my hands until I finally rolled the knot into reach. The herring bag's knot in my right hand I pulled the bag back. Finally, after what seemed like an eternity to me and everyone else in the plane, I was able to drop to my knees on the floor with a herring bag knot in each hand. Ron dropped back into his seat as the planed pitched forward. The pilot was able to trim up for cruise and we headed for Bethel. Holding the herring bags, I spent the one- hour flight kneeling on the floor behind Ron's seat.

I didn't really notice, but the "corner" I had originally grabbed with a pinch had a small tear, through both bags, where my death grip and weight of herring had punched a hole. Herring juice was oozing out onto the floor. I also made my first and last landing without a seatbelt, since I didn't have a hand free to refasten the seatbelt when we arrived in Bethel.

"Well that was a lesson in weight and balance I could've done without." The pilot said when we landed. I could only agree.

A couple years later, I had replaced Dee as Kuskokwim Area Bio, I was helping take the passenger seats out of a 185 at Hagland's Air to make room for a load going to the herring camp at Security Cove. I noticed the floor looked like it was starting to rust through. Aluminum of course doesn't rust so I asked Tom, the pilot/owner about it.

"You remember when that bag of herring nearly killed us? "He asked.

"Yes, only too well." I answered.

"It had a hole in it and herring juice got on the floor. We couldn't get the smell out of the plane. One day, I was taking some batteries up to a mining camp and one of them tipped over and spilled on the floor in that spot. We got it washed off and neutralized before it ate a hole in the floor. And halleluiah, the herring smell was finally gone. Don't try putting any herring into any of my planes again."

COMBAT

Figure 22 Twin Comanche by John Fitzsimmons

Below us I could see large black schools of herring rushing into the shallow water to spawn, north of Atahgo Point on Nunivak Island. Where were you guys last week when the fishery was on. Damn, don't have my herring tube. Be hard to survey from this twin Comanche. The wing is in the way.

Taylor (Sorry I forgot his real name so made this one up.) bumped my shoulder, "That what you're looking for?"

Looking up, I saw a large freighter like ship, less than a half mile offshore, grabbing my binoculars from around my neck I took a look. She was churning up quite a wake, so was definitely underway, the huge gillnet she was fishing with was stung out at a shallow angle as the forward motion fought the drag of the long net. Remembering Paul Cunningham's story of a similar situation in Norton Sound, I said "Let's make some strafing runs, while I take pictures."

"O boy!" Taylor's face lit up like a child on Christmas morning. He banked the Comanche into a diving turn to take us out parallel to the escaping ship then banked into perpendicular strafing run on the hull.

I got my camera off the floor, wishing the old OM-1 had a motor drive, as I raised it to look through and focus the telephoto lens, I had a thought. "Taylor, after our first pass take us in to the nearest beach so we can measure how far offshore she is."

"Roger, here we go."

We raced in on the ship, I began snapping pictures, thumbing the rewind, focusing the camera and adjusting the lens to keep the ship full frame but also try to capture the net filled with sparkling herring and as much of Nunivak Island as possible. We were at wavetop level racing towards the ship, which had huge lettering on the side spelling out JAPAN. Quickly, I was running out of the lens settings, from 210 to 80, my widest view. The ship no longer filled the frame but just JAPAN, I began to wonder when Taylor would pullup. My viewfinder was filled with AN when Taylor began to smoothly raise the plane, he applied just enough back pressure to let us zoom over the deck. The crew running in every direction as I looked down.

"Taylor, we need to measure the distance to the high tide line."

Taylor made a bank out to sea, did a 180, and trimmed the plane for slow flight calling "Time" as we passed the bow. I started the stopwatch function on my watch and a few seconds later stopped it as we crossed the beach.

"Speed?" I called.

"Ninety knots," Taylor replied.

I held my little tape recorder up and turning it on to record with my thumb. I recorded date, location, speed, time, and our names. I would calculate the distance back in the office. I also had a nice complete tape of the evidence if it were needed for an international court case.

"Another pass?" Taylor asked eagerly.

"Yep, can we do another distance on the way in?" I asked.

"OK, how many we going to do?"

"Three defines a point so that would be best. Shit, looks like the bastard cut the net loose." I said. As we zoomed over the shoreline and I started the stopwatch, sure enough, the ship's stern was up, no longer being pulled down by the drag of the net, that they were leaving behind.

As we overtook the ship, stern first, Taylor called out "Bombs away." I stopped the clock and asked for the speed, as we both looked down at the faces looking up at us from the deck below.

"I wish we had a bomb. At least a flour bomb. Bastards, stealing Nunivak's herring." I said as we flew past and Taylor turned for another distance measurement.

"Flour bomb would be fun." He had come in second place at last year's pilot rodeo in Bethel where the local pilots perform a number of flying skills. The flour bombing of a target on the ground was always a real crowd pleaser.

After three passes to get the increasing distance I said "Let's do a low, slow fly-by to see if we can get her name and number." Taylor nodded his head and began a descending turn to set-up a broadside pass. I studied the approaching stern through the 210-lens setting. Ships usually have their name on the stern but this fishing vessel had a ramp for nets built into it so no place for a name. *Wonder how that ramp works in a big following sea? Remember to ask Ken next time you see him.* I had never been chosen as an observer on one of these high-seas fishing vessels. Ken Robinson had great home movies of his stint on the high seas.

We continued along the side and I snapped a picture of the bow where we could read Taiyo Maru 23. (Couldn't remember the name so made it up.) "I heard they always dropped a canvas over their name and number when they came inshore to steal fish. This guy must be a beginner. Guess I better get back. I have people to call."

Taylor nodded. Turning for Bethel and crossing the bows of the Taiyo Maru. He made a base turn then turned final as we made another imaginary torpedo run on the ship. As we buzzed them this time instead of running for cover most of the crew waved their caps at us.

"It's a shame we're harmless. What happens to them now?" Taylor asked.

"I'll call our treaty advisor with the details. He'll call the Coast Guard. They'll probably send a Hercules out of Kodiak to confirm our sighting. I doubt there is a cutter in the area. Not sure who all else he calls. Then the violation goes on the books and will be part of the next treaty negotiations, I think." I said, making a few informed guesses.

"In other words, nothing." He said disgusted.

"Not quite, next time they do the treaty it might be worth dropping the import quota on TVs by a couple of hundred. They always seem to be trading fish for stuff that has nothing to do with fish. I don't get it. Which is why I'm not with the state department." I said.

"Do you have political ambitions?" He said laughing.

"Nope. I'd miss out on making torpedo runs with you." I answered.

Tom was busy flying us home. I began going over what needed to be done, writing a short checklist:

Calculate how far offshore she was.

Call Ron *Write up summary of today's results. Hope there's time for Vera to type. I hate typing.*

Mail film for developing, ask where, will depend on how fast they need it.

Call Coast Guard. Hope Juneau does that.

Whatever else Ron tells me to do.

Call Henry.

I almost forgot Henry, who started all this, he probably won't be happy that the ship is escaping. We drove it off though, it could have stayed catching more of Nunivak's herring. Better ask Henry if he'll try and recover that net. Don't need any more ghost nets killing fish. Plus, they might be able to chop it up into a lot of free herring nets. Henry sure interrupted catching up on my paperwork. That pile from a month in the field from herring season I guess can wait another day. Salmon Working Group meeting tomorrow. Have to prepare for that. Wonder how soon they'll want to open the salmon season? It's too early.

Hope I don't have to veto their decision. That wasn't a simple call this morning. Henry was really in a lather.

I remembered how the day began as the drone of the two engines lulled me into a near nap.

I had answered the phone to a voice saying "Kim, Japanese here catching herring!" I didn't recognize the voice so I had no clue as to who was calling or where "here" was. I asked "Who is this?"

"It's Henry." The voice said.

Henry, which Henry? Got it, I hope. "Henry Ivanoff?" I asked.

"Yes, yes Henry Ivanoff. Japanese fishing, big nets, big ship, do something!"

"OK, Henry calm down, I need more information. Where exactly on Nunivak are, they fishing?"

An exasperated Henry replied, "They fish Cape Manning."

"OK, when did you see them?"

"Need to stop fishing! This morning on way to herring camp."

"OK, sorry for all the questions but the Coast Guard will want to know. Did you get a name or number off the ship?"

"No name, number." *Henry now sounded concerned.*

"That's OK. Think I have what I need. Are you at your house so I can call you back to tell you what's happening?" *Poor guy already had to turn back from herring camp to make the call.*

"Yes. I be here."

"Great, I have to make a couple of calls. Take care. Bye."

The phone clicked off. Telephones are still new. Not much phone etiquette on the Delta yet. I called Ron Regnart, my supervisor first, filled him in and he said, "Nice job. Charter a plane and get out there and photograph that ship. Document its location and if you can get some landmarks in the photos, that helps."

"Which budget should I charge it to?"

"Your herring budget. If Guy gives me a budget code, I'll pass it along." *Ron replied.*

"OK, anything else?"

"Nah, better get the wheels turning on this. Bye, Bye."

"Bye." Don't understand why he says bye bye, just doesn't seem manly enough. Make a note of this budget instruction. He'll hate it when I quote it back when my herring aerial survey budget goes over.

A couple of phone calls latter and I was on my way to the airport to fly out on Executive Air's twin Comache. My first time in this aircraft, quite a step-up from our usual survey planes. The PA-30 was a 6 passenger fast low wing twin engine plane, designed for business travelers. I hoped since we were just trying to spot a ship on the ocean that a fast plane with the extra safety of two engines would work out. It wasn't like I was doing a herring biomass estimate. Plus, it was the only thing available on short notice.

Take off was smooth and we were quickly racing to the coast in the surprising quiet well-appointed cabin. I settled comfortably into the leather upholstered seat. My pilot had just returned from tagging along with his wife to a meeting in Japan and was filling me in on his experiences. Also, his sleep deprivation, he had just gotten off an Alaska Airlines 737, couldn't sleep because of the time zone change, so went to work. Is a pilot suffering jet lag really safe?

We picked up Nunivak Island at Cape Manning flying south looking for our poacher. As Cape Corwin came into view, we could see a large vessel close inshore. A quick check in my binoculars confirmed JAPAN painted in big letters on the hull. Astern they were pulling in a gillnet. We began our "attacks."

I heard Taylor announcing our approach to the Bethel tower and checked my seat belt. The big comfortable Comache set down smoothly. I looked at my watch, set a new record for a fast trip from Cape Corwin. Tom parked and we walked into the office. While I was writing the travel request out, I wondered about the form's name. *Why does anyone accept a "request" as payment? Wonder why they named it that?*

Taylor was already describing our attacks verbally and with his hands to some waiting pilots as I said "Goodbye."

Back at the office I called Ron first. When I got off with Ron, I called Henry and told him the ship was fleeing, but they left a large herring net behind. Since it was still in the water killing fish, it would be a good idea if he and some helpers went down and salvaged it. I offered gas money, figured the budget could handle it. I left a memo describing the mission on Vera's desk to be typed first thing in the morning since it was after 4:30, and I was alone in the office. I took the roll of film out of the camera, dropped in an empty 35mm canister. Weighed it and put it in a heavy-duty envelope addressed to Ron's office so he could get it developed at the 24 hour developers. Ran the envelop through the postage machine. I wasn't completely helpless in the office. In a pinch, I could've typed the memo but it would have been slow. In college once when I was typing a paper at my distribution desk in the Polar Star (University of Alaska's newspaper.) offices. Suse, came out of her neighboring cubicle, pushed me out of my chair, sat down, and whipped out the paper in just a few minutes. Saying "Your slow typing was driving me nuts. I couldn't work!"

As I locked the door to the Bethel office, I remembered the head of the typing pool in Anchorage, telling me about a typist who got smart with Ron when he returned a memo to be retyped because it still had typos in it. She had concluded with "If you want it perfect do it yourself." Ron took her seat and whipped out a perfect copy in less than a minute. "That's how it's done. Can you handle the distribution list?" "Yes Sir," was all she had to say. She hadn't known that Ron had been a clerk in the Army and could type 110 words per minute, error free.

I walked next door to the post office and dropped the film into the out- of-town slot, squatted down, and unlocked our family box, one of the big drawers in the bottom row. This saved us going to the window for all the packages we received. Then drove home in time for supper.

I never found out what happened as a result of our mission. International relations were above my pay-grade.

POLAR BEARS & SIBERIA

*Figure 23 Polar Bear with cubs courtesy
Barbra Dougherty and Pixebay*

"**K**E6628 Nelson Island this is KE6628 Scammon Bay"

"Nelson Island back to caller." Bue replied *His radio technique is getting a little sloppy, like mine. We ever operate a radio in the real world we'll have to clean-up our act. Wonder why they're calling?*

My question was answered almost as fast as it formed, certainly before I finished my bite of scrambled eggs that I had finally gotten to after completing the morning radio schedule. "Is Kim flying today?"

I looked over at Les, our pilot, raising my eyebrows as I chewed. "Just a minute." He said rising with his second cup of coffee in his hand and heading out the door. Doug (Doug Bue, we had four Doug's working in the Bethel office at this time. Doug was usually Bue or Eteg[6], a Yup'ik name the children he had befriended gave him. There isn't a "g" sound in Yup'ik so that was the closest they could come to Doug. Sounded like Douth. It meant anus so was quite amusing to the children.) said into the radio, "Standby one, Scammon."

Les returned as I was biting a strip of bacon in half. "Weather looks CAVU (Clear Air Visibility Unlimited) here."

Looking at Doug I nodded my head in the affirmative not wanting to talk with my mouth full of bacon.

"He's flying. How's the weather there?" Doug being a pilot himself was anticipating their request and Les's first question.

"It's CAVU here with no wind. Could you do an ice check for us. We'd really like to be able to start test fishing. Over."

I ran through my plans for the day and decided there was time. *Bonus, never seen that stretch "my" coast.* "Yes, I'll be happy too." I said after I swallowed.

Doug relayed the message and went through the signing off routine. Les said "Hey, we'll be able to look for that polar bear people have reported."

"Yeah, that would be a treat for me I've only seen them in zoos. Guess there are some advantages to having the Bering Sea freeze so far south this year," I added. Finished my breakfast and did the dishes since it was my turn. Been a weird year. The test fish crew pushing the boat half a mile over the ice to launch. Not sure I would have allowed that but Karen was already doing it when I got

---

[6]   The linguists at the U of A created "new" pronunciation for the alphabet instead of using English pronunciation for reasons they explain in the preface to the Yup' ik dictionary. My knowledge of linguistics wasn't up to the task of understanding why.

here from Goodnews. Good choice making her crew leader this year. Goes to show character is more important that sex or size. Must have been something to see. Her crew-man told me how he wasn't going to drag the boat out on the ice. She just started dragging the Lund out over the ice by herself. After he watched her with the boat, he had been shamed into joining her. Can't believe that tiny woman could even move that boat.

Dishes done; I collected my survey maps, putting them on the clip board. Along with my herring tube, a piece of plastic plumbing pipe with a piece of transparency paper inserted in a slot at one end. The paper had a grid printed on it, lastly stuck to the side with self-adhesive Velcro was a clinometer. By recording the plane's altitude, angle of observation and the known size of the base from the grid, you add a little geometry and calculate the size of the herring school. There was a table for conversion to biomass based on water depth and the surface area of the herring school. I also carried a stop watch since sometimes the schools were longer than the tube could measure. Then using the time and speed of plane you calculated the length of the school. The herring biologists who worked all this out in Bristol Bay years ago, they had a purse seiner standing by to catch the whole school so they could convert area and water depth into biomass. When you "finished" the aerial part of the survey you still had to sit down with all the data recorded, a calculator, the charts of the area (for depth of ocean) and the tables of biomass vs surface area/depth. When doing career days at the local school I used this example as why math was important to aspiring biologists. Usually a great disappointment to people who thought the job was just scuba diving and watching fish from watching TV.

Les had already left to preflight the plane while I was doing dishes. With my survey gear and a bag of bite sized Snickers bars I headed up to the Toksook Bay Airport. Ready for a day of flying. My survival bag, small duffle with sleeping bag, ELT (emergency locator beacon), camp stove inside a small cooking pot, and granola bars, was already in the plane.

Toksook's airport had been blasted and bulldozed out of Nelson Island's rocky steep surface. The island didn't have a lot of flat places. At one end they must have set up a rock crusher to grind the broken rock into gravel to surface the runway. The construction left a pit in the rock that was now the village dump. We saw it regularly since if your deposit in the honey bucket filled it, you were responsible for sealing the plastic bag full of feces and urine, replacing it with a new bag and hauling the full bag to the dump with the three-wheeler and its trailer. The bag was usually very full snice to avoid this unpleasant task people had a very poor understanding of "full."

Les was already waiting in the Cessna 185 and I just climbed into the seat next to him. Buckled myself in while Les was going through the startup. As I put my headphones on and adjusted the voice actuated mike, he taxied the plane out onto the runway. Toksook like most villages had an uncontrolled airport so Les announced our intentions on the airport's traffic channel. Pushed the throttle to full and we accelerated down the gravel runway. He applied a little forward pressure and the tail came up. As I had discovered learning to fly a "tail-dragger" this control move is a little contrary to your instincts. Lowering the nose while on the ground looking through a spinning prop, seems wrong. Instinctively you think the prop will hit the ground. Once you get the feel for it though it really doesn't require much forward pressure, you just sort of follow the control yoke forward as the tail starts flying, you apply enough pressure to keep it from settling back, gravity is the law, not an option. As always, Les handled things smoothly and we quickly reached airspeed, a little back pressure and the nose rose and we left the ground. On gravel runways lift off is always a relief, since the rattle of gravel off various surfaces of the plane stops. I always worried about damage, but it always seemed to be limited to paint chips.

We turned over the village and Les leveled out at 1,200 feet, the ideal altitude for the herring tube and we followed the coastline mostly west. Out to Cape Vancouver, the tip of Nelson Island. The survey conditions were still poor. Ice break-up had left the water roiled and murky, my chances of seeing a school of herring were zip. I said into the mike "Les, this water is still a mess. Can't see a thing. We can speed up and scout for clear water on our way to Scammon Bay. Les adjusted the trim tab just in time for the Cape's usual turbulent air greeting. Even at 1,200 feet the

Cape created katabatic winds and air turbulence that continued down to the water. It could be quite disruptive to both flight and boating if the winds were strong. We got bounced around a bit but nothing serious. Les made a wide turn, out over Etolin Strait to minimize the turbulence. The strait had many ice bergs from the breaking up of the Bering Sea ice to the north. We followed the coast into Tununak Bay and over the village of the same name. Same muddy water so we continued following the coast past Newtok to Kumlunak Peninsula the southern end of Hazen Bay. Also, the western boundary of Kuskokwim Area, where I managed the commercial and subsistence fisheries. Now I was seeing new geography. On the coast between Hazen and Hooper Bays, we spotted the sow polar bear and her two half grown cubs walking north on the shore ice.

We circled, descending to get a better look." Wow, wonder how they made it past so many villages without getting shot." Les said.

"The fuel barge is late because of the ice. Probably no one's getting out. No gas for snowgos. Be my guess." We were circling the little family much lower now and they broke into a run.

"Oops, to close." Les said pulling the plane up into a gentle climb. "You get any good pictures?"

"I think so but never really know until the film comes back. (I didn't.) If they are any good, I'll give you copies. Surprising how white they are even with all this mud. Sheep in Iowa were always a dingy gray with dirt, even when it was dry."

"Yeah, but they don't have to sneak-up on grass." Les replied.

Laughing I said "Yeah, seals are more observant than grass. I think sheep avoid swimming."

"There's Cape Romanzof. Looks like Scammon Bay is still frozen." Les said as we approached our goal.

"Let's take a swing around so I can give a full ice report. I've never been here before. Closest I ever got wasn't years ago picking-up fish tickets at Black River."

"There's a processor at Black River?" Les asked.

"Yes or at least there was, Mr. Amocan (sp?) had a plant where they salt cured salmon. Real gentleman with a great memory. It's been fourteen or fifteen years since I was there but he remembered me when he came to the ADF&G booth at fish expo in Seattle a couple of years ago. Took me to lunch at his club there. Real class act."

"Seen enough ice?" Les asked.

"Yep, looks like it will be a couple of days before they do any test fishing."

"Would you like to swing by Black River for old times' sake? I've never been there." Les asked.

"Sure. I've never seen that stretch of coast between here and there. Maybe we'll see another polar bear. I said.

"Or Siberia. I bet as clear as it is today, we can get high enough to see it?"

"Nose bleed altitude here we come." I answered. As Les began to climb as we followed the coast north. Since we were high enough to glide back to land if the engine failed, Les creeped out over the Bering Sea to get us a little closer to Siberia. As we climbed through 9,000 feet, we could see either a cloud bank or Siberia. A rough calculation back at the office came up with the horizon should have been about 120 miles away. The Chukchi Peninsula, the nearest part of Siberia, was over 300 miles. So, we didn't see Siberia, probably St. Mathew Island. A part of my area I never did see. It's uninhabited. There is a blue king crab fishery in the ocean surrounding it but that was managed by the Westward Region in Kodiak. I asked Ron once about getting the fishery shifted to Bethel. I thought it would add a little more variety to my job. He said the red king crab fishery in Norton

Sound (handled by the Nome office) was already too much trouble and he was letting me add more.

Sightseeing over and water conditions making herring surveys impossible, we took a short cut across the delta back to Toksook Bay. Our home away from home until herring season was over. Never did make it back to Black River.

IMPATIECE CAN KILL

Figure 24 Cessna 185Mark Pilkington<u>www.skywagons.com</u>

Back in Toksook things followed the usual pattern. Our test fishing began to catch herring ready to spawn. We had meetings where fishers brought in herring samples, processors' techs broke them open to remove the eggs, the weight of the eggs divided by the weight of the herring gave the "roe percentage." "Beach Parties" as they were known in the rest of the state were new in the Kuskokwim Area. I introduced them in the Kuskokwim Area as a way for the fishers and processors to be involved in the sometimes-controversial decision of when to fish. Had to change the name to beach meeting after the first one in Goodnews Bay because a bunch of fishers arrived with booze ready to party.

The roe was the target of the fishery and the industry set the price based on 10% roe by body weight. Once fishing began each fisher's delivery of herring would be sampled and they would be paid based on the roe percentage. Every tenth of a percent higher than 10% roe received a higher price and inversely every tenth below resulted in a reduced price. Depending on the market, if the roe percentage was less than 6 to 8 percent, the fisher would receive a rock bottom "bait herring" price. The purpose of the meetings was to try and time the commercial openings to achieve the highest price. Ten percent roe by weight was rare in the Bering Sea since the herring spawn at an older age and much larger size than further south. We believed this was because the colder water caused herring to have a shorter growing season. It took more growing seasons to gain enough extra energy to "invest" a large part of a fish's energy budget in spawning.

Samples finally were high enough that processors and fishers agreed it was time to fish. Herring come into the beach to spawn on eel grass or kelp with the incoming tide. They get carried away in their excited state and spawn on rocks, sand, shells just about anything that gets in the way. The spawned out and exhausted herring usually hitchhike back to sea on the outgoing tide. We announced the commercial opening for the six hours of incoming tide. Of course, if the total harvest was approaching the guideline, we reduced the number of hours fishing. We collected verbal reports and fish tickets after every opening to keep a running tally of the harvest.

In addition, we flew biomass surveys, weather, and water visibility allowing. If the surveys showed more herring than the population model had predicted before the season, then we increased the harvest guideline. Our survey results were of great interest in-season. The regional herring research staff found them of great interest postseason since they were the starting point for calculating the following year's herring biomass and harvest guideline.

Wind, fog, clouds, and turbulent water had prevented any good estimates of the herring biomass from the air as the catch approached the guideline. The CB and VHF radio was filled with calls asking/demanding we do a survey. People walked into the office constantly asking/demanding we do survey. Processors arrived from their ships in helicopters demanding a survey. Les and I were becoming tired of the constant accusations that we weren't flying because we were lazy, didn't care, or were scared. Not quite sure where the line is between insanity and sensibility, herring season always forced exploring that boundary.

Finally, the weather broke and turned clear as a high-pressure system moved in. Unfortunately, air flows from high too low like water (it is just a thin liquid). The recently departed low was still very close. We had clear skies but high winds.

The clear sky increased the demands for survey results. I knew that the high winds would continue to keep water visibility poor since the resulting turbulent water would be turbid. Les couldn't take hounding and walked out to check on the plane and weather. He returned a few minutes later as I was telling a caller on the CB that we were going to try and fly today.

"We can do it. Let's go." Les said.

"OK, happy to give it a try. At least I can get away from the radio." I replied as I began gathering my survey gear.

Doug Bue, pilot and long-time seasonal employee said, "Kim, do you think the water will have settled yet?"

"Probably not, but can't hurt to look. Good for people to see the plane in the air." I replied. I followed Les into the Arctic entryway where our coats hung along with the odor of the seal and walrus meat that had been stored there during the winter. Took my Mustang Float Jacket down and put it on before stepping out into the wind.

Les asked, "Do you really think that will help?"

"Not sure. If you have to ditch at sea, unless there's a boat close, I'm probably screwed. I tried getting out from under an overturned skiff in a float coat in Ketchikan once. Pretty much impossible. Figure in a sinking airplane, it would trap you in the plane. If I make it to the surface, I might keep suffering from cold water for half an hour instead of six minutes. If we go down on land, the Mustang's neoprene "beaver-tail" might keep me from hypothermia longer than you. Unless there's a fire and all these synthetic fabrics burn like a torch. Survival is really about picking a good pilot and well-maintained plane. But shit happens and the extras can't hurt."

"Well, you got that right. Adventures usually are a result of poor planning or panic. "Les said."

As we arrived at the airport. The Cessna 185 was tied securely to the ground but the wind made it quiver as it struggled to blow/fly away. Les climbed in saying" I warmed the engine up earlier so it should fire right up. You untie us after I start and stay away from the meat chopper."

Les started the engine, locked the brakes as I quickly untied the left wing, tail and right wing followed by jumping into the right-hand passenger seat. Les used brakes and throttle to position the plane. Then broadcasted our intentions on the radio. With a roar, the engine started us down the runway. The tail seemed to lift almost immediately since the wind was nearly fast enough to provide takeoff speed. We left the ground quickly with all the "extra" airspeed provided by the strong wind. Suddenly the world spun. The left wing rose to vertical while I watched the right wing's tip almost graze the ground. A vison of cartwheeling down the runway flashed through my mind. Then we swung back into our normal attitude and continued our climb.

I looked at Les, who had a very intense expression on his face and said, "Nice save. This wing tip almost scraped the runway. Good thing we weren't a foot lower."

"Damn squirrely winds on this island. Better get on the radio." He announced turbulent winds on the airport channel and reported them to Bethel.

We turned and began following the shoreline at the village looking for herring. Saw the test fish crew struggling with the wind as they launched the skiff. The water was the color of coffee with cream. The high winds had stirred-up the bottom sediments well. We got bounced pretty good by turbulence all along the way. As we approached Cape Vancouver, famous for creating katabatic winds, I said "Let's skip the Cape today."

"I was about to suggest that."

We turned out over the water as Les climbed high enough to avoid turbulence caused by the Cape. "Les, we're wasting time. The water is to turbid for a survey. We should just land."

"Standby." Les tuned in to the latest weather from Bethel FAA. The wind was supposed to lessen as the day continued. "Let's keep trying. It's that or go back to Bethel. I'm not landing at Toksook until the wind drops."

"OK. Let's take a look at the Tununak side. We don't need to fly at survey altitude or speed unless I see some clear water. If the wind is still blowing, we can take a look at the east side of Nunivak. It should be mostly in the lee"

"OK." Les said.

We cruised the Hazen Bay side of Nelson Island more comfortably at 1,500 feet, above the ground turbulence. The water was even worse on this side. "Les, we're wasting our time here, let's try Nunivak." I said.

"Where do you want to start?"

Forgot to think about that. I looked at the black and white copy of the navigation chart on my clip board. "Let's try Cape Etolin. That shore is pretty rocky so the water might be clear." We crossed the strait and picked up the Nunivak shoreline at Cape Etolin flying east then turning south at

Cape Manning. We passed an anchored processor, who didn't seem to be taking any deliveries. Most of the fishers were camped on a nearby beach. The water visibility was better but I wasn't sure if it was clear enough to see herring or not, since I wasn't seeing any. Not quite halfway to Cape Corwin, I saw the unmistakable dark creamy white color of herring spawning but I couldn't see the school of herring. "Les, I can't see herring so let's go back. Could you see if you can raise Icicle, that processor we passed on the radio and tell them about this spawning going on."

"Got em. They said 'Thank you'. What's up? You usually let them do their own spotting?"

"They don't have a plane or chopper this year. Fishermen can't seem to get onto the herring over here. Weird they (the herring) don't seem to be all rushing the beach at once on Nunivak. Just drips and drabs. Hope this spawn is the start of the big one. How's the wind?"

"It's dropped. ERA just took an Otter (ERA used twin Otters a lot.) In and out. Reported some turbulence but nothing serious. Guess we don't get to spend the night back in Bethel."

"Rats. Guess I get to spend the rest of the day explaining why we didn't get a herring survey."

TAKEOFF CONTEST

Figure 25 DeHavilland DHC 6 Twin Otter
by Raimund Stehmann Wikipedia

The herring camp at Security Cove was located in USFWS Alaska Maritime National Wildlife Refuge. The herring fishery in the Cove predated the refuge by years. When the new Refuge Manager had been flying his domain, a big job since it extended way out on the Aleutian Island chain, he saw what we left at the herring camp during the off-season and was unhappy. There was a shed/steam-bath we had built out of drift logs and lumber. We stored the wall-tent frame and floors along with some other odds and ends in and around it. While the camp was operating, it served as the bathing facility since there was no running water on the beach. We didn't care to do polar bear plunges into the ocean to clean our carcasses. Over the years, a number of empty 55-gallon drums, that we weighted down to prevent blowing away, had accumulated. We used the gas from the drums in our outboards and to refuel the survey plane. The stove oil drums ran our heater. Our intention was to fly them back and collect the deposit but it seemed at the end of the herring season the budget and time for empty barrel charters was always used up so we never got around to returning the drums to the dealer in Bethel.

The Refuge Manager found the camp very unsightly and a violation of the wilderness status of the area. I received an angry phone call about it shortly after I became the Kuskokwim Area biologist. Luckily, my previous job as the ANILCA (Alaska National Interest Lands Conservation Act) coordinator meant I knew more about the act than the new Refuge Manager. When he said we had to cease and desist use and return everything to its original condition I explained we were exempted and allowed to carry on activities necessary to manage the natural resources. He hung-up with a "We'll see about that."

His next call was friendlier. He asked if we couldn't clean-up the unsightly old gas drums? I told him it was in the operational plan but we had failed to do it. We would do it this year when we set-up camp instead of waiting until the end of the season. He thanked me.

So that first spring day my assistant, Keith, Doug, our seasonal troubleshooter and I flew down with Däg (Dog) Hansen. I asked Dog \ about his unusual first name. "I'm from Norway. Went to sea on a freighter to see the world. Discovered that English speakers can't pronounce an a with an umlaut. You either say Dag or Dog. When I learned to fly in Australia, I was working on a sheep station. Dag is what they call ewe's afterbirth. I decided to be Dog with English speakers."

"Wow. Sounds like you have seen the world. How do you pronounce your name in Norwegian?

"Däg" he said "it means sun."

Which fit since he was a blond, tall, slender and handsome man, or so the female staff told me. With the sound of the roaring 185's engine in the background, I spent the next few minutes trying to say his name properly.

A frustrated Dog finally said "Thanks for trying but it's just not possible for English speakers. Dog is fine."

"OK, I hate to misprounce someone's name but I am getting used to it. Yup'ik names often tie my tongue in knots. Your English is perfect, where did you learn?"

"In school in Norway. They thought I sounded North American in Australia. Not sure why people expect me to sound like what passes for a Norwegian accent in this country."

"Movies and TV mostly. But if you're from the Midwest like me, you've probably heard the Sons of Norway from Minnesota or North Dakota. They speak in a Norwegian accent lots of the time. If you've seen the movie Fargo, they use the Minnesota version, a little exaggerated."

"Yeah, that's what my girlfriend told me. I can't imagine a Norwegian speaking English like that."

"You sound like a girl I knew in college from Sweden. Her English was perfect and she was embarrassed by her relatives in Des Moines who, in her words, "Talk like they just got off the boat." That's Security Cove coming up. Looks like we might be a little early. Hope the tide is out far enough for you to land." Dog and I had been conversing on the pair of voice actuated headsets Hagland's had added to the 185 so pilot and passenger didn't have to shout over the engine. Doug and Keith were in the backseat unable to hear us.

"Looks like there's enough room. That's a huge beach."

"Yeah, but that sand above the tideline is too soft. We usually land on the damp sand after the tide goes out."

"OK, Tom told me. I'll drag it and see. Switching to the radio." When he switched, I could hear both sides of the conversation but my voice connection was blocked. Dog announced our intention to land to any aircraft in the area. Then swung over the high side of the beach, the steam bath still had the floors, 2"x4" frames with two sheets of plywood nailed to them, producing a 4'x8' rectangle. We used the rectangles to make a floor for the Weatherport where we lived and the wall tent where we sampled herring. It beat trying to live and work on loose sand.

"There's enough solid sand next to the water but I'll still test it first." Dog said as he turned a short downwind leg and set-up on his final. As I used to do with my T-cart on skis on undisturbed snow, he took us down but as the wheels touched instead of actually landing, he hit the power and ran the wheels down the expected runway. On snow this trick accomplished several things. First, you packed down a track to land on so you didn't sink in deep snow. Not as important for landing as taking off; it's hard to accelerate through soft snow. If there were any unseen irregularities, like logs or rocks, the plane would bounce into the air which since you were already at flight speed was harmless. Then you looked for a smoother spot.

Sand was different. You could tell by the resistance if the sand was too soft to land and takeoff safely. If the sand or snow is too soft and you commit to a full landing the plane stops so suddenly it usually ends up on its nose or upside down. Dog ran down a stretch of beach long enough to take-off safely. "It's good," he announced and entered into a low landing pattern over the beach. Checking to be sure there's enough runway for takeoff is also very important. Landing doesn't require as much space as taking off. There's an old saying,"Any landing you can walk away from is a good one." I believe any landing you can takeoff from is a great one.

Once on the ground we all climbed out, stretching. Doug and Keith had done this before. Even though I was "in charge" this was my first time. I said, "Keith, it's your show. What's next?"

"You wanted to send back empty barrels on the return flight so were early. The Otter will be here in half an hour or so. Let's see how many barrels and floorboards we can get down here before he comes."

Doug was already above the high tide line, looking and pacing. As we walked up the beach towards him and the shed, he picked-up a driftwood stick about 6' long and stuck it in the ground between us and the shed. "I think we have enough level space here for the Weatherport."

"OK, let's get barrels and floorboards." Keith replied.

Doug joined the two of us as we trudged through the soft sand. I was a little surprised when Dog caught up and joined us while we were untying and unwrapping the floorboards which had been secured to the shed/steam-bath.

"Plane's safe. What can I do?" This was unexpected, pilots are hired to fly usually they sit in the plane until the work is done. Keith and Doug were busy with knots and walking the lines around the floorboards and the shed.

I said "As soon as there free we need to carry the floorboards down to that stick Doug stuck in the sand. If there's time before the Otter comes, we need to round-up these old barrels so we can send a load of them back on the Otter."

Doug and Keith had a floorboard between them and were heading down the beach. Dog and I each grabbed an end of the next floorboard and followed. The operation went pretty quickly and, at Doug's direction, we roughly put the floorboards down to make the floor for the Weatherport and wall tent. We decided that tightening and leveling could wait and we went after empty drums.

Most of the drums were in one place sort of piled behind the steam-bath. One of the ropes had come loose so we had a few drums that the wind had moved around the beach. We worked on the pile that was still tied together. We got all ten or fifteen of them down to the landing area by the time the ERA Otter landed on the beach.

We unloaded the Otter, taking out the Weatherport, inflatable skiff, outboard motor, wall-tent, a drum of fuel oil, a drum of gas, a couple of drums of aviation gas, radios, and other necessities. The reasons none of us could fly with the load was there was gas on board. At that time the FFA had a regulation that fuel and passengers couldn't fly together. Unless, of course, the fuel was in the plane's FAA certified tanks.

In spite of the temperature in the low forties, the three of us were down to T-shirts and sweating. Our pilots had taken a walk beachcombing for glass balls and other treasures. The glass balls came from the Japanese high seas fishing fleet which uses them as net floats. I was told they actually make them as needed on the ship.

As we finished, they returned in a friendly discussion of which plane the twin Otter or the 185 could takeoff in the shortest distance. We were asked to be the judges. Keith and Doug had stationed themselves down the "runway" with sticks to mark the takeoff spots. I scratched out a starting line with my bootheel and the Otter jockeyed into position with the nosewheel on the line. He locked his brakes, bringing the engines up to what sounded like full throttle. The locked wheels were actually skidding forward a little when he released the brakes. I expected him to raise the nosewheel quickly but instead it was obvious he was actually using down elevator to hold it on the beach as he accelerated. Then he raised the main-wheels first, reducing the drag of two wheels while keeping the nosewheel on the ground before finishing the takeoff. Doug ran in from the side marking the end of the tracks left by both the nosewheel and mains. *Didn't think to ask which wheel was a takeoff. Have to* discuss that.

Dog moved the 185 up to the line stopping on my signal. He locked the brakes and increased the throttle to takeoff. His tires started to inch forward in spite of the brakes, too. He released the brakes and raised the tail ASAP, the now streamlined plane raced down the beach and broke with the ground heading north, behind the Otter for Bethel. His propwash scattered Doug's sticks.

Keith marked the 185's takeoff point. I was following the wheel tracks up the beach to see the results. The two planes had to our surprise left the ground very close together. With Doug's sticks gone we were having trouble deciphering the tracks. Pretty much a tie, but the 185 had won by less than three feet. Since the Otter had a load of empty drums, they didn't all fit in, we called it a tie.

The next day, Tom Hagland landed with Joni Snellgrove, Security Cove's crew leader, and with odds and ends for the camp that hadn't made the first flights. The camp was set-up. Keith and I left Joni and Doug in charge and climbed into the plane with Tom for a short flight to Platinum so we could set up camp there. A simpler task since we rented space in the Chevron warehouse. On the way, Tom asked "Kim, will it be OK if Dog is your contract pilot for the herring season?"

"O yeah. I was impressed with his flying and he seems to fit right in. Tell him he tied with the Otter"

BOAT COUNT

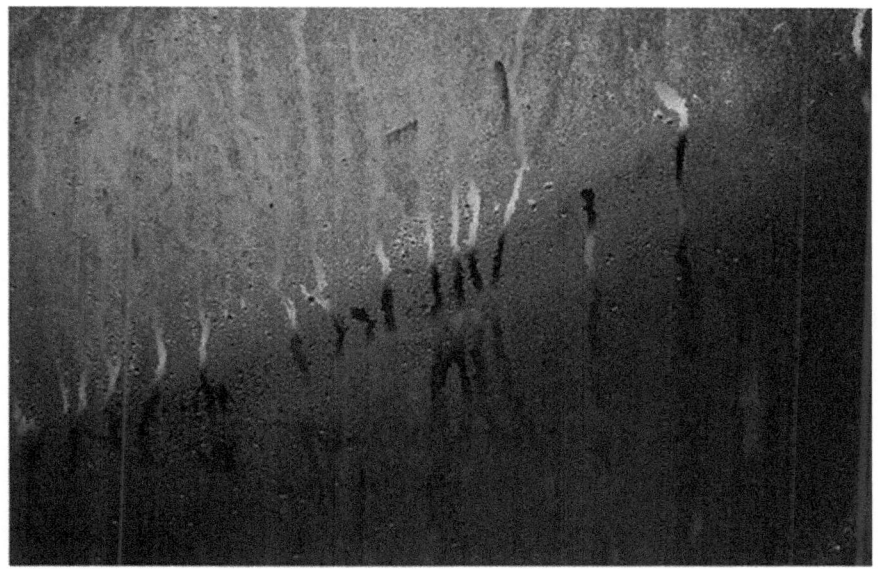

*Figure 26 Imagine blood spatter and spray rolling down
a windscreen. Image by Pexels courtesy Pixabay*

My job description as Kuskokwim Area biologist included "other duties as assigned." A catch all phrase included in most if not all of the department's job descriptions. At the start of the salmon season one year, the fishers and processors were at loggerheads over the price of salmon. King salmon escapement had been a developing problem so the staff and I were rather relieved by the continuing negotiations since the fishers didn't want the fishery opened. We weren't constantly fielding calls telling us the river was full of fish and it was time to open.

The three processors were another matter, they wanted an opening because they were sure the commercial fishers would break the strike given the chance. Finally, test fishing catches and historical run timing made it impossible not to open the fishery since the majority of the catch would be chum salmon. The processors of course thought their lobbying not biology had gotten the wished-for opening. The fishers were convinced we were in the processors' pocket. The phone wouldn't stop ringing as one angry fisher after another called to blame us. Business as usual except instead of demanding an opening they were demanding it stay closed.

My phone rang again and I reluctantly turned to answer it. *O it's line 3. Must be Ron or Juneau. Hope its Ron. (*Line 3 was a private number so our supervisors could always get through.) "Hello, it's Kim."

"Are you Mr. Francisco?"

"Yes, who's this?" Calling on our private number and where did you get it?

"Hello Mr. Francisco. This is Thor Clausen (Yes, I made this one up.) with the Department of Labor. We have a request from the Kuskokwim Fishermen's Cooperative to mediate the contract dispute they are having. Your HQ says there hasn't been an opening yet. Is that right?"

"Yes Sir. We announced the first opening for Thursday morning."

"So, the fishers haven't been on strike yet."

"They announced they were on strike, gee couple weeks ago I think."

"Yes, but they haven't actually not fished because they were on strike but rather because fishing was closed."

"Yes, that's right. Guess I hadn't thought of it that way. This is my first strike."

"I want to give you my number. Then please notify me if more than 50% of the fisher's don't fish."

"Hmm, alright, but the processors have 36 hours to turn in the fish tickets and it takes us a day or so to process them so we can get an effort count."

"Can't you just fly out and count the boats fishing and compare to what historically the number would be. That's the way it's usually done."

"Yeah, we can do that. Don't really have boat counts in the aerial survey budget. Do you have a budget code I can charge it too?"

"No, this is your responsibility."

Our responsibility! You're the Department of Labor, not Commercial. Fisheries. O well. "OK, I'll check with my boss. If he's OK with it, I'll do it."

"I'm sure it will be all right." Thor said.

I got his number and we said our goodbyes. I called Ron and he said "Yes, damn it, we pay for them to do their jobs. Be thankful they don't make you mediate the contract or charge us for their travel."

Wednesday was hell with people calling wanting to know why we weren't honoring the strike and keeping fishing closed down. At least we had a new answer, you can't be on strike if you can't fish. It didn't go over very well. In Yup'ik culture things are done by consensus so we were out of order. Between phone calls, I worked up the average levels of effort for the last five and ten years. Along with the maximum and minimum levels.

Then I thought maybe they wanted the mode (most frequently occurring number) instead of the mean (average). So, I worked up the modes too, which were virtually the same as the means. Meanwhile, word got out, incorrectly, that it would be me deciding if they were on strike or not. People stormed into the office and called. telling me to tell Labor they were on strike. Went through a lot of antacid and aspirin during that 24 hours.

A small committee of leaders from the Coop came to convince me to close the fishery. I explained once again that wasn't our job. Rather, we were to provide fishing opportunity that insured sustained yield. I would be flying the fishery and counting the boats fishing. Then I would give the count to the Department of Labor and they would determine if it was a strike. I gave them a copy of the historical effort numbers I had worked-up and Faxed to Thor.

"How will you tell if they are fishing or just us out there telling people not to fish?" One asked.

"I won't count them unless they have a net in the water. I wanted to wait for fish tickets but Labor didn't want wait."

We went over the same questions asked different ways for about forty-five minutes. The meeting concluded with "We'll have boats on the river counting too, you better count right."

The commercial fishing period began at one. I was out at Hagland's and in the air at two. Today, we weren't doing any beach or gravel bar landings so we took one of the Cessna 207s that usually were used for runway to runway flying between villages. It was a nice day, calm winds, a few puffy cumulus clouds, virtually unlimited visibility. The upstream boundary for the first opening was at Bethel, cutting District 1 in half protecting the kings that had all readied passed. So, we started just upstream of Bethel. The management plan for the Kuskokwim had recently been changed, at the staff and my suggestion, because of the king salmon escapement problem. Given their migrating speed, about 15 miles a day, this allowed an extra three days' worth of fish to escape.

"It's looking like they really are striking." I commented to Tom as we came up on Napaskiak.

"Yeah, haven't seen many boats fishing mostly just guys running around."

"Probably checking who isn't striking. Or making sure strikebreakers know someone is watching. "Well, the river is getting wider now. Going to have to start using the binoculars more." I commented

THUNK!

The engine faltered, then regained its normal rhythm. *What was that! Engine failure? Are we going down? O shit what a bloody mess!* As I turned from the side window to windscreen my view was completely blocked by blood, bloody white feathers, and various organs, pieces of intestine sliding up the plexiglass, pushed by the prop wash up over the top.

"Looks like a gull. The engine and prop alright?" I asked while simultaneously doing an instrument scan of the panel. *Everything looks OK.*

"Yeah. Engine seems fine. Can't tell about the prop till we inspect it on the ground. Right now, it seems alright. Damn I didn't file an IFR flight plan." Tom joked. (Instrument Flight Rules, poor visibility means you work with airports and their radar as well as your instruments to keep on course.) Landing still requires minimum visibility.

Tom was trying to see through the windshield as was I. The big pieces of the bird had blown off but the blood seemed to be spreading into every corner of the windscreen effectively painting it red.

"Going to have to land to wash the windshield. Probably should inspect the prop before we fly much more. We're heading back." Tom said as he turned north west towards the Bethel airport. He got on the radio and called the tower and explained his situation. They took over announcing the emergency to the planes waiting in the pattern. Giving Tom instructions to bring us safety into the pattern and lining up on the runway. I sat watching, impressed at Tom's skill holding the plane on course then descending for the landing. But as we approached the ground he said quietly, I think he forgot the voice actuated mike he was wearing, "Shit, I need a horizon." Luckily, he was wrong. His skill allowed him to make a gentle descent onto the runway using the artificial horizon and other instruments and what little he could see through the blood and out the side. With no horizon he didn't flare, but gently brought the plane in in a slightly nose high attitude. When the main wheels hit the runway, he dropped the nose. A modified wheel landing. Then, as we taxied back to Hagland's hanger, he was a little embarrassed since the lack of forward vision caused him to put on quite a show as he wiggled the plane slowly back to the hanger. All the wiggling was needed to see where we were going out the side windows.

As we wiggled along, I said "Now we know what it was like for Lindberg, the Spirit didn't have a windshield."

"Yeah, always thought that was a mistake. Now I know it was."

Thor seemed to drag his feet about coming to Bethel to mediate. The effort count which I finished after helping with the task of washing dried blood off the windscreen. Clearly showed the fishers were on strike, it wasn't "officially" a strike until we had a second period during which effort dropped even more. The mediation went quickly after that, the strike was settled and things returned to normal. Fishers wanting to know why we weren't letting them fish more to makeup the lost time and why I hadn't supported the strike.

PANTHER II+

Figure 27 Quad City Challenger (not a Panther 2+ but similar except it can be flown safety) by Rusty qcaircraft.com

The dream of building my own plane lived on. I read every issue of the EAA magazine from cover to cover. Priced Republics, Cubs, Stinsons, Taylorcrafts and anything else I thought might be affordable. But life and my salary in Ketchikan and Anchorage at 0 geographic differential just didn't let me add another plane to my life. (The state of Alaska's salary schedule was divided into nine geographic districts. Each district received, above the base, a percentage increase based on the cost of living in that area. Bethel was range 8.) Then we moved to Bethel, between my annual performance increases and the geographic differential there was money to spare. Thanks to Marsha's frugal ways and listening to old time Bethelites, we learned to make barge orders and do lots of shopping when my job took me to Anchorage. Lastly, discovered living in Bethel prevented buying beer, stopping at Fred Myers or other Department stores and buying things on impulse on the way home from work. After the first year, even after taxes, it looked like a plane might be affordable.

I found several plane kits I was interested in. When I had first began considering my own homebuilt you had to buy plans and work from scratch. A new industry had arisen where you bought a kit that included everything you needed. In some cases, the kits included preassembled parts. I created a spreadsheet for comparison of the kits I was interested in and finally ended up with two possibilities, a Kit Fox or Panther II+. Comparing the two, I decided the Kit Fox required some building skills that might challenge my skill set plus it was a little more expensive. Lastly, but importantly, it required longer to build. I made a chart comparing the two, sat down with Marsha. "I want you to help with choosing which plane kit I get to build."

"What if I don't want you to build a plane?"

"Well, I, hmm, didn't really think of that. Do you want me to buy a used plane?"

"No, I don't want another plane. Remember what happened before."

"The Taylorcraft was a good plane and we made money when we sold it. A kit plane would be different from the Luscombe since it would be a brand-new when we start. Since I built it, I can work on it so we'll save on mechanic's fees." I reminded her.

"Where would you build the plane?"

"Since the garage isn't heated, I measured the living room and I can do it here."

"I'll have a plane in my living room all winter!"

After several days "discussion" and I finally got her to agree. I think she really thought a winter with a living room filled with plane pieces was better than me buying a used one.

The first box of the kit arrived and I tore right into it. Every free moment was spent assembling, bolting and pop riveting the wings together. I actually had them done and moved into the garage before the fuselage kit arrived. Getting the wings out of the living room and into the garage was quite the circus. I hadn't really planned how I would get them around the right-angled turns required by our Arctic entry ways. My friend, John Morgart helped, by lifting the tips high, John was really tall, the base all the way to the floor and tilting them as perpendicular as they would go, we got them out without any disassembly.

The fuselage box arrived next and I considered how I would get it out while assembling. I completed as much of the cabin as possible. Then moved it to the garage. Then completed the empennage, the "tube" behind the cabin that attaches to the tail. In the case of the Panther, it actually was a tube so there was only a few attachment points and guides for the control cables to attach.

Assembling the tail required a little more effort since like the wings the tubing frame had to be assembled. The guides and pulleys for the control cables added the cables and then the fabric skin stretched over. Of course, there were hinges for the rudder and elevator. The finished tail required a little fancy maneuvering through the doors. Since the horizontal stabilizer had to be mostly vertical to get through the doors which made the vertical stabilizer, now in a horizontal position, wider than the corners of the door. It took a lot of jockeying to find the right position that the tail fit through the door. I had picked a "warm" day, temperature was in the twenty-degree range (Fahrenheit), so the furnace didn't run a lot extra.

With a catalytic white gas-fueled tent warmer, I managed to complete the fuselage assembly in the garage with frequent breaks to warm my hands. The plane had been designed to have its wings attached last at an airport or some other roomy spot so you could hanger the plane at home then tow to the airport to fly. I waited for the engine box. Becoming impatient, I called a couple of times to check and see if it had been shipped. I was told they were so busy and shorthanded that it hadn't been crated yet but they would be shipping it soon.

In the meantime, I had written up a short note for "This Is What I'm Building" column for the EAA Magazine's Sport Plane (This was before the internet.). Shortly after it appeared, I received a postcard urging me to call ASAP about the Panther 2+. The number belonged to an AMT (The special, FAA approved aircraft mechanic certification.) So, I assumed he would know what he was talking about. I talked to a soft-spoken man who was very concerned for my safety. He had been hired to build a Panther for a man who had bought the kit but didn't have time to assemble it. When completed, the mechanic had test flown the finished plane. The test flight started well but the controls lost effectiveness as the flight continued. Concerned, he had landed and begun inspecting the plane. The many pivot points that allowed the control cables to turn corners were seriously bent and required replacement. He warned me if I wanted a safe aircraft, I would have to obtain a sheet of special steel. He rattled off the steel specifications that I hastily jotted down. Then take all the pivot pieces and trace them out on the steel, cut them out, and drill the attachment holes in them. Replacing everyone with the new stronger steel pieces. I thanked him and said goodbye and sat thoughtfully. *How did this happen again? Why hadn't any other builder reported this problem? Would I need to hire a machinist or mechanic? Were my tools up to the job? O Boy! I get to buy new tools. Marsha won't like that.*

I turned on the TV and watched a recording of Big Fish Downunder to take my mind off of the mess. Then I sat down with the plans and found every pivot point and circled it in red. There were a lot of them. The plans included an illustration of both a blown-up one and an actual sized one so the kit builder could pick them out of the bag of parts when called for. I began doing some checking on what getting a machine shop, there weren't any in Bethel, to do the job or what it would take for me to do it.

I knew a mechanic from the gun club who said he would help. Just as I was preparing to pull the trigger and buy the steel, I thought to call the company and demand replacements. If that failed, I would order the steel and start on replacement pivot arms. The phone went unanswered when I tried calling several times. I continued calling day after day, until a thick letter arrived registered mail with a return receipt attached. The Panther company had gone bankrupt. There was a long list of secured creditors who would be paid first when the assets were sold. Then a list of unsecured creditors which would be paid after the secured creditors with whatever was left. My name was about midway down the list of unsecured creditors.

I called the company number again and there was no answer. I was encouraged that the phone still rang so continued calling and did finally reach someone. I asked if the engine box had been shipped before the bankruptcy. The man said, "I don't think so but I'll check." There were background noises that I interrupted as a file drawer opening and a search for a file going on. He continued as he searched, "We quit buying engines when the money began running out so unless we already had it, we wouldn't have shipped it. Here it is. No, I'm sorry you'll have to wait until all this is settled, or buy an engine and put it in yourself.

"I already paid for the engine, why am I an unsecured creditor?"

"Good question, you'll have to ask the judge. Goodbye."

Shit, should I contact a lawyer? Nah, probably good money after bad. Surely the court knows what it is doing. Wonder who pays for all this registered mail? Have to find out what a ROTEC engine costs? Check where I can get a piece of that steel. Wonder how hard it is to cut and drill? Probably at least need to borrow Jerry's drill press, after I get them cutout. Check yellow pages?

Looking at the yellow pages in the back of our Anchorage phonebook I discovered there were more steamship companies listed than steel distributors. There two of them, one each in Anchorage and Fairbanks. *Hey stupid. Jerry cut out and made those steel silhouette targets for the shooting club. I'll just take a copy of the design to the shoot Sunday. He'll know where to get the steel and help me do this.*

Next stop was my collection of EAA magazines. I checked the ads for ROTEC engines adapted for aircraft use. They were less than regular aircraft engines, like Continental and Lycoming but I was going to be spending a lot more than I had told Marsha I would. *This is going to take another long discussion; she doesn't get the flying thing.*

It wasn't pleasant but Marsha did finally say go ahead, very reluctantly. I was feeling like a jerk who had forced her go along to shut me up. I used the argument that a flying plane would be sellable and we might get some of our money back.

Ron Perry, the Yukon Refuge Manager (The Yukon Refuge is headquartered in Bethel and is actually composed of the Yukon-Kuskokwim Delta, the Kuskokwim has always been the ugly one with the great personality who gets left home.) and I were talking about the Civilian Air Patrol getting started in Bethel. He had gotten approval for them to use an empty bay in the USFWS hanger at the airport. But the poor young people didn't have a plane to learn in.

BINGO! "Ron could you ask if they would be interested in my homebuilt. The company went bankrupt so they aren't sending the engine box. An aviation mechanic who built one said it isn't safe to fly. But it would be great to use for ground training and basics in control use. I'd be happy to donate it." *At least get a tax break out of this fiasco.*

"Kim, I'll ask."

A day or two later, Ron called and told me the CAP was really excited to have the plane. They showed up with a couple of pickups and hauled off the Panther 2+ and all the directions so they could finish it. The last time I saw it, it was hanging from the ceiling of the CAP's side of the FWS hanger without an engine. I hope it helped some young people to follow their aviation dream.

BETHEL FLYING CLUB

Figure 28 Cessna 172 on floats similar to Bethel Flying Club's. curtesy of Andre Cantin THABET AEROPLUS

Kincaid, our new FWP (Fish& Wildlife Protection, a Division of the Alaska Department of Public Safety) sergeant stationed in Bethel, dropped by one morning and said "Kim have I got a deal for you."

Usually those words are a signal to hide your wallet and call an attorney. But I had come to trust Mike during our brief friendship so I listened cautiously. He and his wife had a sign on their door "Our Dogs are more Important than Guests." You have to trust people like that.

"You said you can't afford to own a plane anymore. I found a beautiful 172 including floats that I can't afford but if several of us go-in together it would be affordable. We form the Bethel Flying Club and when you fly you pay for gas. Otherwise, we just split the maintence costs evenly. We all agree that any damage done to the plane while we're flying it, we have to pay for ourselves. That way we only need liability insurance. What do you think?"

I had checked around for flying clubs and didn't find any in Bethel. This could work. "Yeah sounds like a great idea. I'll have to talk to Marsha of course. Who else is interested?"

"The new blue shirt, Warren (My apologies, I've forgotten both he and his wife's name. Made these up.) with you that's three and if I can find one more, we make membership $6,500. That will cover the plane and give us a little slush fund for insurance. I don't think we want more than four, otherwise we'll always be working out who gets to use the plane on weekends."

Charlie, my assistant, stuck his head in the door. "Sorry, I couldn't help overhearing. Have to talk to Tricia but I'd like to be the fourth."

Mike said, "I didn't know you were a pilot?"

"I'm not but thought this would be a chance to learn. "Charlie replied.

"Yeah, Cessna 172 is a great trainer. You'll need an instructor."

"There's a couple of guys in town that can teach. They just don't have planes insured for flying lessons and told me I needed my own," Charlie explained.

"Great! You guys talk to your wives and let me know. Got to go." Mike headed out the door.

Tricia and Marsha were persuaded to go along. Marsha and I soon owned a quarter of a Cessna 172 on floats. It was summer so Mike had flown the plane back from Anchorage with the landing gear as luggage, which was a good thing since floats are really expensive to ship.

Mr. Satler, one of the plane-less instructors in town, was my float brush-up teacher. I hadn't flown on floats for a while and didn't feel ready to solo. I picked it right back up. As I recall, it only took an hour or two of instruction for me to "brush-up" my float rating.

Marsha was not a flyer. She was prone to airsickness even on big commercial jets. She never got sick when I was flying but I think that was because she was too scared to get sick. After I had a successful fishing trip, she decided to give the 172 a try.

Out at H-Marker lake, Bethel's Floatplane pond, I untied and pushed the plane off the mud beach, then using the lines on the floats to move it to the loading dock. Then loaded the gear into the plane and did the walk around, checking the oil, looking for damage and, as always with floatplanes, pumping the floats. The 172's floats had a convenient one-way valve on a standpipe leading to the bottom of the floats. You pulled out the red ball sealing the top of the pipe and just put the pump down into the opening, the pump's suction would raise any water that had leaked or condensed into the float compartment up and spit it out over the side. I've forgotten how many compartments there were but I pumped them all out in both floats. Didn't get much water from any of them since we had a pair of good tight floats. In older floats, like on my Luscombe, there was an inspection plate over each compartment, instead of just testing for the small amounts of water with the pump you had to unscrew, open, and visually look for water with a flashlight. If you found any, you put the pump into the inspection hole and pumped it out. Then you replaced the inspection plate making sure not to damage the seal. It was very time consuming and the standpipe system was vastly superior.

Remembering the old pilot's saying, "You can't use the runway behind you." Marsha and I taxied to the far downwind end of the lake. During the taxi, I performed the preflight engine runup where you test carburetor heat, throttle, and magnetos. Everything checked out so using the float and plane rudders and a burst of power to create enough airflow over the rudder I made 180⁰ turn, without losing to much takeoff room but being super cautious with Marsha aboard, I throttled way back so the wind could push us back to the edge of the Lilly pads. Then lifted the rudders, added full throttle and 20 degrees of flaps, the nose came up and spray flew as the power caused the plane to sit back on its heels. We quickly accelerated, the nose coming down level as the floats rose up on step. We accelerated down the lake as we reached the green line, takeoff speed, I pulled back on the yoke to break us free from the water. We stayed on the pond. We were halfway across the pond, still plenty of room to takeoff. We continued to gain speed, I tried an old trick, that I had been taught was unnecessary with modern planes and added some right alerion with some corrective rudder to keep us on a straight line, to try and raise the right float out of the water first. We stayed glued to the lake. I throttled down and turned the plane around as soon as it came off the step. I added throttle to step taxi back to our starting point. The turn and step taxi had the desired effect of covering the glassy water surface with small waves. Glassy water sometimes develops so much dynamic tension that it holds the floats on the pond. I had never experienced it before but had heard of it and thought this must be the problem. I explained to Marsha as I turned back into the wind accelerating onto step, the waves break the water's tension allowing the floats to break free. Once again, we raced down the lake on step, reaching takeoff speed I once again tried to break the floats free. The plane stubbornly refused to fly! More speed I thought. Letting the acceleration increase our speed. Still the plane wouldn't life off. "Shit." I pulled the throttle back along with the yoke to raise the nose. Floatplanes don't have brakes so I hoped by raising the nose and tips of the floats I would create more drag that would slow us faster. It did but the upwind shore continued to loom ominously closer.

What looks like a solid shoreline on H-Marker is actually floating moss growing out over and on top of the water. We coasted into the moss. Shutting down the engine I pulled up my hip boots and climbed out of the plane. Telling Marsha "I'll get us turned around. Then will taxi back to the dock to see if I can figure out what is wrong."

"I'm not flying anywhere in this plane. You just take me home."

"Yes dear."

"How many times have I told you not to say that." She replied as we started one of our recurring exchanges about "Yes dear."

I had dropped onto the float and into the moss, discovering the water under the moss was way deeper than my hip boots. Half expecting this, I had kept a firm hold on the float. *Now what? You're supposed to roll out of these bogs but that won't move the plane. Wish I had one of those reversible props, could just back out the tracks we cut. Wonder if I can swim us out?* I pulled myself over the float then on to the first cross strut between the floats and under the engine. Once I was centered, I began kicking as hard as I could. Slowly, the floats and plane began to move back through the two cuts in the moss they had made coming in. The light wind pushing the plane out probably helped a little, too. As the plane gained momentum, we began gaining speed and my job became a little easier. Although kicking in the water in full hip boots was still very tiring. In spite of the cold water on my legs, my face and upper body were soaked in sweat by the time the plane finally moved out the moss. *That will teach you to abort your* takeoffs sooner.

I moved back across the cross strut to the float and tried to pull myself up on to it. My first try was unsuccessful. There just wasn't anything to get a good grip on. *If you pull yourself up to the bow, your weight will probably push it down enough you could crawl on to it. Now, give this one* more try.

Grabbing the float's forward cleat, I gave a mighty heave while kicking the water with my remaining strength. I was able to get high enough that I straddled the float and got both palms down flat on the top of the float. I paused to rest but realized quickly that my weight combined with the weight of two hip boots full of water was a real strain on my arms and shoulders. I made a quick grab aft and up with my left, supporting myself with just my right arm on the float and got the cross brace between the vertical struts that had the steps into the plane on it. Doing a one-armed pullup, I got my right hand on to the same step strut. I was able to pull both knees up onto the float. Thankfully not catching my crotch on the cleat. Finally, supported by my arms and legs I was able to take a little breather. Then shifted myself around so I sitting, on the float, there was too much water in the waders to bend my knees so I just leaned back holding the step and raised my legs. The water poured out of the tops of my hip boots soaking my already wet butt. Lighter, by I don't know how many pounds, I was able to stand and roll the tops of the boots down to my ankles. I climbed dripping into the plane.

"Why do you always go in over your boots? Don't you pay any attention." Marsha demanded.

"Marsha, ask anybody, they've never made a pair of hip boots tall enough. That's why we have chest waders. Anyway, the water under the moss was too deep to wade. I had to swim us out."

"Swim us out? What do you mean?" She asked.

Marsha's mind isn't mechanical and I never could explain how something was done to her. I had to show her. I said, "I'll show you latter. Right now, we need to buckle-up. I think the wind has blown us far enough out that I can taxi us in to our parking place."

I started the engine and with full rudder, on the plane and floats, was able to turn us towards the beach. I almost ended up in the moss again as we curved forward. I hadn't been as far out as I thought the turn took us very close to the edge of the moss.

It was a short taxi to our parking place and, with a burst of throttle I was able to slide the plane up through the mud so our tie down weights were under the wings. The public (free) floatplane beach was really just a stretch of muddy shoreline. Everyone had their own tie down weights they had lugged into "their" position on the shore.

I locked the controls in neutral so the wind couldn't move the alerions, rudder and elevator. Also checked to be sure the flaps were locked up. Marsha was busy packing our gear back to the truck through the muddy beach.

I got out my multitool, opening the Phillips screw driver head and began removing the inspection plates on the floats, peering in with the flashlight we kept in the plane. The center, main compartment of the right float was full of water. *No wonder I couldn't take off. But I pumped it. Why is it full? Should I leave it full for Kincaid to see or pump it out. We're self-supported in this club,* it's your responsibility.

I put the pump on the standpipe and couldn't get any water out. I put the pump into the compartment through the inspection plate and pumped it out. Marsha came back from her last trip to the truck. "Can we go now the mosquitos are terrible?"

"Just a minute. I think I found the problem and should be able to fix it."

"You can't work on planes?"

"Your right. The owner can't do big stuff, has to be a certified mechanic. But this is a little owner allowed maintence problem."

"Well, I'm waiting in the truck to get out of these bugs." She said marching off. I watched her go. Cute butt in hip boots. They kind of setoff her little bum. Back to the float or you won't have any blood left. Deet will take care of that.

After slathering on a heavy coating of bug juice which stopped the less determined mosquitos, I looked at the bottom of the standpipe with the flashlight. *Yep, crap blocking it. Wish Marsha had stayed. I could use someone to hold the flashlight.*

I went to work clearing the bottom of the pipe. When the clog looked clear, I looked desperately for a water container. There was nothing in the plane or on the ground nearby. *I don't want to go back to the truck. I'll have to explain to Marsha. She'll want to go home. The float pump!* I grabbed the pump from on top of the float and waded into the lake, sucking the pump full then returning to the float inspection hole. Put the discharge hose in the inspection hole and pressed down sending a pump full of water into the float. Then reversing the pump, I tried to pump it out. I didn't get much. *Probably not enough water.* I filled and emptied the pump several times then tried again. *Shit! It's still clogged. I could bring my drain snake back but I don't think it will fit, too big. Guess I could use a rifle cleaning rod or maybe a coat hanger? Talk to Mike, he flies floats all the time. Maybe he's run into this* problem before.

I put the inspection plate back and locked up the plane. On the way home Marsha delivered another "I told you so speech" about planes and plane ownership. Several times reminding me "You always say it's cheaper and safer to charter a plane when you need it."

Yeah, but you always say I don't need it. Thought if we had our own you would want it used. What I said was "This club is like chartering, we have to pay rent every time we fly, we just don't have to pay for a pilot."

Mike hadn't run into the problem before. While I was working on the honey-do list to make peace that afternoon, he drove out and using a wire was able to get the clog out.

The Bethel Flying Club came to an end that winter. Charlie was practicing touch and goes on wheels as part of his pilot training and lost control on a go. Damages to the plane were $25,000, almost what the four of us had paid for the plane. He paid for the repairs as agreed but sold his share to the trooper. who then offered to buy everyone's shares. I did, reluctantly, sell and Marsha was happy.

ICE

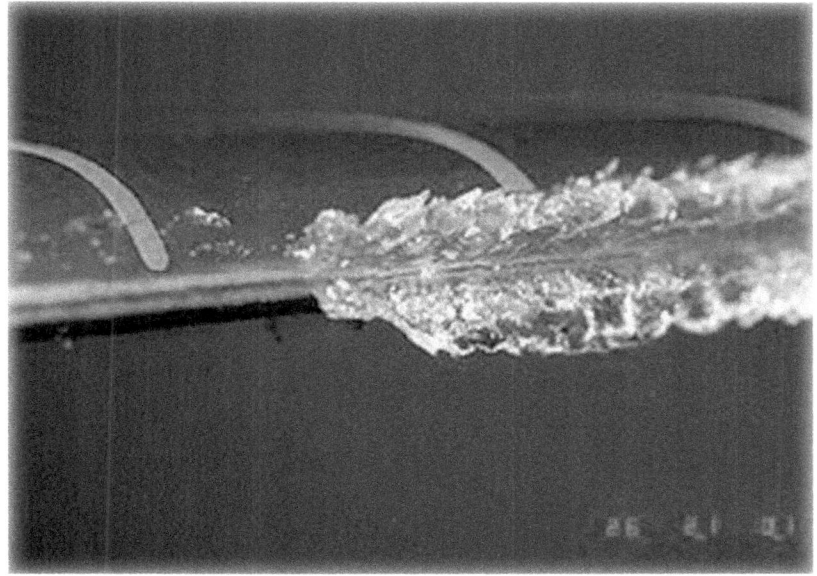

Figure 29 Icing on wing. Wikimedia Creative Commons

My mind was a jumble of herring and salmon issues as I tried to think of what to do about the Nunivak district, would the Nelson Island district go over harvest guideline while I was in town, and what to say at the Kuskokwim Salmon Management Group that evening. It was a crummy day, visibility just barely the legal mile, low ceiling and not a lot to see between Toksook and Bethel.

"What's wrong?" Dick said. (Not Dick Hamlin mentioned earlier. I'm ashamed Dick's last name has escaped me. He was a friend, good neighbor and favorite pilot for my final years in Bethel. Sadly, he and our Wildlife Biologist died in a crash doing a moose survey a few months after I retired.)

"Something's wrong?" I said, looking up from my lap and automatically doing an instrument sweep. Dick was working the controls and trim.

"Yeah, look at that ice." Dick said.

The windscreen and plane's cowling had been collecting ice and then shedding it for a while but now it was just building up. I unfastened my seatbelt and raised myself up so my head was between the dashboard and windscreen. Turning left and right I could see part of the leading edge of both wings which also had a thickening layer of ice. As I sat back down buckling the seatbelt I said "Yeah and it's on the wings too."

Dick said, a little concern in his voice, "Yeah I tried to climb, usually a little warmer higher and it comes off. But it got worse. We'll try descending, sometimes that gets it off. I won't declare an emergency yet but start watching for places to set down."

I appreciated his vote of confidence in choosing a landing spot but could already see his eyes were searching the ground for places already. I was worried.

In training, they tell you about icing on the plane and in the carburetor. I had experienced carburetor ice, everyone did, the engine rpms drop and you pull the carb heat knob out and on. Your rpms comeback up and life is good. I knew icing on the plane was possible but except for seeing some come off the wing of jet air liners I'd been in, I had never experienced ice in a small plane. There are deicing systems on larger commercial planes and even some of the high-end private aircraft. Their cost and added weight made them a rarity in bush planes.

Ice is triple trouble on airplanes. The added weight can take a plane past its load limit. But at the same time, the ice is adding weight it destroys the wings lift, reducing load carrying capacity. Finally, ice increases drag.

The drag slows the plane further reducing lift. The result is the plane can only do one thing; go down.

Dick and I were flying under a 500' ceiling which didn't leave a lot of room or options for finding a safe landing spot or as Dick hoped slightly warmer temperatures that would release the ice. As we began descending, Dick called into Bethel FAA, "This is 04293, about 50 miles west of Bethel in route from Toksook. We are experiencing severe icing."

"Bethel back to 04293, do you have an emergency?"

"93 back. Not yet, descending looking for warmer air. 93 out." Dick concentrated on flying which I could tell was becoming harder. He added some flaps to increase lift. Our altitude was down to 300' but ice kept building.

I was busy watching the ice for any sign it was warming and breaking off. There wasn't any. We passed through 250'. *When will he declare an emergency? My imagination or we've quit* building ice?

We passed through 200'.

Dick is sweating. Don't think I've ever seen that before. There's 150'. He's picked up the mike."

"SWISH"

The top half, the thinnest ice, on the windscreen slipped off. Dick hesitated with the mike.

"SWOSH"

There goes the ice on the bottom half. We can see again.

"CRACK CRASH"

We both jumped as the ice on the cowling came free and crashed into the windscreen.

"CRACK SWOSH"

The plane rocked as the most of the ice on the right wing came off. Dick had to add alerion and rudder to level the wings as the right wing rose and the left sunk. The mike hung where he had dropped it so he could fly.

Weird how it goes in chunks. You'd think it would just melt off. Plane's surfaces must warm faster than the ice so it just breaks loose under stress of slipstream pressure.

"CRACK CRASH"

The plane rocked again as Dick corrected back for the shift in weight as the ice on the left wing broke off, crashing into the rudder.

"Glad that's over. He wagged the plane with the rudder to test for damage. "Guess cruising altitude to Bethel is 100' today." Dick said with a smile of relief on his face.

"Hey, a hundred feet beats zero any day." I added.

After my arrival and departure for the office, Hagland's mechanic and Dick gave the 185 a close inspection for ice damage. There wasn't any. Early the next morning Dick and I returned to Toksook.

THUNDERSTORMS

Figure 30 Storm Clouds. Free Image cdm.
pixabay.com Creative Commons.

The Yukon Delta Refuge includes thirty-seven villages, and the property they received in ANILCA. Calista, the Regional Native Corporation also has inholdings as do a number of mines. It also includes commercial fisheries for salmon, herring, halibut and a number of freshwater species managed by the State of Alaska. Most U.S.F.W.S. refuges have no or very few inholdings or commercial activities as a result refuge managers are not use to working with other managers. The refuge manager when I became area biologist had wanted every commercial fisher to get individual permits from the refuge, in addition to the state licensing requirements. He also had other conflicts with ADFG and the private inholdings. Unlike his predecessor, the new Yukon Delta Refuge Manager Ron Perry, visited me in his first days; after introducing himself he said, "After seeing the file full of letters, phone logs, and U.S.F.W.S. solicitor letters between my predecessor, you, and Assistant Attorney General for Alaska can we just start over?." We both have roughly the same mission here and not enough people to do the job. If we work together, wherever possible, we'll both do a better job.""

I replied. "That's all I wanted from the beginning. Welcome to the Delta."

Sitting down Ron said "Yeah, saw that in your first memo but I was afraid you might hold a grudge." Ron replied.

"Nope, job is way too big for grudges." I replied. The result was a long productive partnership and friendship between us, personally, and the A.D.F.&G. and U.S.F.W.S. Which was so unusual, the partnership between agencies, that a few years later U.S.F.W.S. in Washington actually hired a team of consultants to come out and study us to try and explain how and why we worked so well together. I never saw the final report. Ron and I both discussed their hours of time-wasting interviews. They clearly were frustrated by Ron, Sam (The wildlife biologist, not sure if they interviewed our Subsistence Division.) and I seemingly parroting the same thing "It's too big a job to do alone." I'm sure they were too well paid to hand in a one page one-line report.

As a result, many years later I found myself in a U.S.F.W.S. Super Cub being flown by Rick, a pilot/biologist. Rick had received mixed reviews as a pilot from my various contacts but I wasn't too concerned. I had flown with him enough times that I was confident in his skill. I was more concerned about the Fed's safety regulations requiring a helmet and Nomex overalls. This particular July day was warmer than normal. The fireproof Nomex overalls didn't breathe and were uncomfortably hot. I quickly had discovered on earlier flights that the helmet made surveys impossible. The face bubble constantly collided with the side windows preventing looking down out of the plane. The chief pilot, George, and I reached an agreement, I would wear the helmet on takeoffs and landings but could take it off while surveying as long as I kept it handy to be pulled on if crashing was imminent. Neither of us expected that to ever happen.

Most of the salmon streams were upstream of the Refuge, but FWS provided plane and pilot for the streams on the Refuge. Rick and I started on the Tuluksak River, the last salmon index tributary, going upstream, that was both in the Refuge and the Kuskokwim Area. I was already soaking my clothes inside the overalls. *Wish I had just worn my underwear.* The Tuluksak is a snake of a river, not a popular survey with the staff. I usually did it since before becoming area biologist I had conducted a habitat evaluation on the stream as a result of complaints from the village of Tuluksak, located at the confluence of the river with the Kuskokwim. The cause of the complaints was the reactivation of a gold dredge in the upper Tuluksak river. They had some trouble with their setting ponds that had resulted in polluting the river with silt in violation of their permit to operate in a salmon stream. As a result, I knew the stream well and sort of enjoyed having my insides wrenched about while surveying it.

Rick and I started at the downstream boundary of index area 101. This portion of the stream is out on the delta so the topography is very flat and filled with lakes and ponds of various sizes and colors. Always found the different colors of the delta ponds interesting. Evidently, I was the only one since I could never convince anyone that it would be worth finding out why. But I digress, just put that in to show some of the thoughts that rambled around in my head as I sat in the backseat of a Super Cub slowly traveling from one stream to the next. Once over the stream, there was not much time for anything but the survey.

Area 101's banks are delta silt, thawed by the warmer river water. There is a narrow band often only one tree wide, of spruce trees using this thawed soil for their roots. Beyond the trees is the frozen permafrost, wet muskeg with ponds and lakes. As a result of the thawed eroding silt banks this portion of the river is usually unsurveyable due to water turbidity. So, we flew in a straight line, skipping the river bends until the water cleared as the geology of its bed changed to sand and gravel. Once we reached clear water, we started following every twist and turn of the river as I began counting, mostly migrating salmon here since most of the streambed was still too full of fines (silt and sand) to build a successful redd. (Salmon nest, the eggs require water flowing through the gravel for oxygen. Silt and sand are to tight to allow flow.) Surveys are easier in a Super Cub since they are slow by design and handle pretty well at the lower survey speeds we use. I had Rick fly at 800 feet following the river bank. Since the fuselage of a cub is so narrow, I could just turn my head and look out the opposite window to keep my eyes on the stream. In larger planes, I usually sat in the backseat sliding from side to side to keep my eyes on the stream, as Regnart had taught me. Using both sides eased the pilot's burden since less severe turns were required to keep my eyes on the stream. Sharp steep banked curves, while exciting, invite a phenomenon known as the accelerated stall. The steepness of the bank can cause the wing's angle of attack to exceed what is needed to fly. Resulting in a stall, turning the plane into a rock.

"Twenty chum, two king, fifty chum, 1 king, 40 chum, water still a little turbid chum hard to see chums, 12 king, ten no fifteen chum" I was speaking into a handheld tape recorder, noting the salmon I saw and also survey conditions for playback latter. "Thirty-five chum, two kings, WHAT THE HELL." The plane had suddenly flipped as we entered an accelerated stall. *We're going to die!* My instincts and training kicked in and I pulled the seat and shoulder harness tight. *Helmet!* I saw the throttle on the left side of my seat go full forward. *Nose down full throttle. Right recovery. Not enough room to reach flight speed.* I was simultaneously grabbing the helmet from where it was wedged between my hip and the fuselage and pushing it over my head. My stomach was trying to escape out of my throat. I wasn't breathing and pretty sure my heart stopped too. *Why is this taking so long? We don't have that much altitude!* I was fumbling with the helmet straps trying to get them fastened. The nose began rising suddenly, I quit fumbling and looked out over Rick's tense shoulders at the river, the view slipping from water to gravel bar becoming trees. *Careful release back stick before secondary stall. Trees better than ground.* Rick raised nose. *Not* too much!

SWISH SNAP SWISH SNAP!

The floats went through the trees. *Please nothing big enough to stop us.* We burst quickly out of the thin line of trees and the Delta's muskeg spread out before us. There was a lake almost dead ahead. I breathed. I thanked God. I was starting to thank Rick when he added flaps and reduced throttle. *We're landing. Shut up till were on the water.* Rick smoothly put the plane down. Shut off the engine and took a deep breath sitting back in his seat. I put my hand on his shoulder "Nice job, you sure saved our asses. The rest of us too." He didn't laugh just nodded.

"Let's stretch." Rick said.

"Good idea." I unfastened the door on the right side. Dropping the bottom half to where it snapped onto the fuselage. Then snapped the top half up. "Do you want step out first?" I asked a little uncertain of my legs.

"Go ahead."

Leaving my helmet on the seat I climbed out onto the float. Stretched, enjoying the beautiful view of the Kilbuck Mountains. Rick unfastened his seat belt and swung his legs around to the door. The two of us moving around was making the plane rock as it drifted on the lake so I steadied myself with a hand on the fuselage while unzipping the overalls to let some cool air in. Rick stretched then walking forward said "I need a piss."

"Good idea." I turned to the stern and with our backs to each other we got rid of the mornings coffee that suddenly was an unbearable burden.

We finished, both standing silently with our thoughts. I thanked God again. Not sure how much time passed, not much, and Rick asked "Ready to start again?"

"Yep, do you know where we left off?"

"Exactly. Just have to look for the broken tree tops." He said with a forced laugh.

I gave a little chuckle. "Nice job of flying." I repeated as I climbed into the plane. "Does time slowdown in emergencies for you? It always does for me.

"Yeah, thanks, didn't start out good but we finished all right."

We picked up at the bend where disaster had nearly ended our lives and my tape continued "12 kin gs, 40 chums, 1 king Otter Creek, home of the turbobeavers, begin area 102, 5 kings, 37 chum…"

Otter Creek was one of the Tuluksak's larger tributaries. From its headwaters in the mountains it flows out into the Delta so its lower reaches meander through the muskeg before reaching the larger river. Like many such streams it picks up a tannic brown stain that colors the water, which is still clear just brown. It does hinder visibility, chum salmon in particular due to their unique spawning colors disappear in it. But unlike silt it is not a problem for aquatic life. The stream was home to many beavers. As soon as the pond behind one dam ended there was another dam. All these dams settled out any fines washing down stream which is why the water was clear only stained.

Kim Sundburg, Habitat Division and I (His wife, Debbie Clausen, once called me "the cheap imitation" when she called Kim's office and I answered.) started the investigation of the village complaint and the miner's first explanation was "the beavers in Otter Creek caused it." Kim S. replied "Well, they must be turbo-beavers." Listening to the playback of the tapes gets tedious and it helped me to add a little commentary to change the subject "Otter Creek. home of the turbo beavers.).

Back to the Tuluksak survey "5 king, 25 chums, Wha" the survey stopped there because Rick said "Look at that. We can't fly into that."

Looking up I saw a huge cumulonimbus (thunderstorm if you haven't had weather training) lighting flashing and rain pouring down. The entire river valley from mountainside to mountainside was blocked. It was really beautiful, all that raw power on display. *Wow, didn't realize I missed thunderstorms. Only one I remember in Bethel during the last eleven years. Of course, up here in the mountains they're common.* I leaned forward to Rick's shoulder and shouted over the engine "Yep, can't finish here let's try the Kwethluk."

"OK, where do you want to start?" Rick replied as he turned south.

I unclipped the xeroxed map of Tuluksak's index areas and put it on the bottom of the stack of maps on the clipboard. Pulled out the nav chart with the index areas from the bottom of the stack, some pilots could relate to our xeroxed topo maps, others had to have a nav chart. Rather than find out if they could or not while flying, I just always had a nav chart marked with the index areas. I put it over Rick's shoulder pointing out the downstream edge of area 102 on the Kwethluk. "Here would be great."

"What about 101?" Rick asked.

"It's always to turbid, so we don't survey it anymore." Rick nodded and set a course for the Kwethluk.

We arrived and as I expected visibility at the beginning of 102 was impossible but it quickly improved and I began the monotonous counting.

"There's Denny." Rick announced over his shoulder.

Sure enough, Dennis Strom, Deputy Refuge Manager, was running his boat upriver filled with people and gear. Dennis was a good friend and hunting buddy; he hadn't mentioned making a Kwethluk trip. "What's he up too?" I asked.

"He took the day off to work on that church camp." Rick answered.

"O yeah." I said remembering Dennis had mentioned that the congregation was refurbishing the camp for a summer youth church camp. I had continued my counts, including "Denny's boat" on my tape for variety.

"Shit" I heard from up front. An expletive you don't like hearing from pilots, doctors and surgeons.

Looking up there was another mountain-to-mountain cumulonimbus blocking our way. I pulled my chart out, refolding, handed it over Rick's shoulder. "Let's try the Eek, unless we're low on gas. Wonder if these thunderstorms are in all of the mountain passes?"

"Gas is good. Eek here we come."

We resumed a southerly heading crosscountry picking up the Eek and commenced our third survey of the morning. We made it to index area 103 water clarity was good. Rick was flying a tight corner in a narrow pass in the mountains when suddenly we were slammed towards one side of the narrow gorge. Looking up, I saw Rick hard at work trying to recover control of the plane as the windscreen was covered in rain. He made a tight 180 ° turn, buffeted by turbulence, the rocky mountain side came into view out of the rain just as the plane began to repond to the controls. We narrowly escaped the pass. Downstream, we immediately broke out into the sunshine. What a welcomed sight.

"Nice job. Let's call it a day. They can't say we didn't try." I called over the engine to Rick. He nodded in the affirmative and set a course for H-marker lake. I noted discontinuing due to thunderstorms on my tape. Sitting back wondering how a guy could see around a corner in the mountains. *A guy could get rich if he invented an instrument to see around corners. Above my pay grade.* I began eating my lunch, it was a long way to Bethel. *Going to have to try again tomorrow.* Weather allowing.

We arrived at H-marker and Rick setup for a landing on the mirror like lake. As the plane set down something happened. The floats began skipping like a flat stone, sideways to our direction of travel! Bouncing across the water, Rick and I were both frozen. I don't think either of us had ever heard of or experienced such a thing. Rick kept back pressure on the stick to hold the nose up, applying alerion to hold the left wing down, trying to keep the right out of the water. His hand hovered uncertainly over the throttle.

Power? Maybe? Don't think so. Shit, what to do? Never heard of this happening. Probably no one lived to tell tale. Please God forgive me. My mind was whirling, near death experiences have always made time crawl for me. But I couldn't think of anything to suggest that Rick wasn't doing.

In emergencies, things that happen in an instant seem to last forever. My hypothesis is that the mind slips into overdrive which causes time to pass slowly. Like high speed photography. I've met other people, who when asked said the same thing happens to them. Most I've asked don't know what I'm talking about.

We continued skipping across the lake, which isn't really big to begin with, the shoreline was approaching fast as I watched through the side window which had become the windscreen, when it wasn't blocked by the wing reaching for the water. *When are we going to tip over? Hope I can keep a firm hold on the frame through the crash. If I can, it will help me find my way out if we sink.*

SWOSH

The plane settled into the water on its floats, tipping precariously, the right wing almost catching the water. Then upright and we were safe. Rick didn't speak. He dropped the water rudders, added a little power and turned the plane towards the dock. It was suddenly really hot. As we approached the dock, I opened the door. Rick killed the engine and coasted right up to the dock. I jumped out grabbing the float's bowline. "Do you want my help pulling her up?"

Rick said "No just push me off."

"OK" I said pushing him back out into the lake. He waited in the plane thoughtfully, I walked back to the truck with my clipboard and lunch sack. The truck cab was hot from the sun. I rolled down the windows. Found the giant-sized SNICKERS candy bar in my lunch and opened it with difficulty because of shaking useless hands. I began munching and thinking. Wish I drove "Tunes" the radio would be nice now. Why doesn't fear happen until your safe? Barry didn't cover that in his column on the growth of the fear lobe. Guess mine

must finally be done. I don't want to fly surveys anymore. Today flat scared me, three times or four? Use to be having a new story of almost dying was just another great story to tell over coffee. Guess we kind of did that to show how tough we were. Alden[7] was right, you don't have to risk your life to enjoy flying. If my math is right, I could have retired in April. I'll check with Marsha and Personnel, then write the memo. Can hear the Regional staff celebrating now. Probably all the fishers out here too. Hands look pretty good now. Shaking seems to be over. Candy bar is gone, better use this sugar rush to drive. I put the truck in gear and let out the clutch successfully. Yep, I can drive. Doug can't do surveys but Charlie still enjoys them. Cindy too. Think I can avoid any more while Marsha and I make our plans. Course Cindy will have her hands full managing Coho's. It was a good idea to let them each take a fishery this summer, in case I retired. Region is supposed to be paying attention to how they do. Wait to see how she does before I decide which one to recommend. Here's the office. Cheated death again. How true.

---

[7] Alden Williams was a pilot who I had the pleasure of having coffee with once in Emmonak. He had started bush flying in Alaska with Noel Wein in the 1920's or 30's. He stayed with Wein Airlines until he reached mandatory retirement age. Then returned to bush flying. He had tens of thousands of hours of flying and never "bent" an airplane.

LAST SURVEY

Figure 31 Plane Crash Nunivak Island airport. Francisco Photo.

The pilot spun the round trim control again. This time backing it up and really slamming it down. "Damn it, trim tabs are frozen." *Shit, this was supposed to be a nice simple muskox and reindeer count. No twisting streams. Nothing dangerous. Now I'm going to die a month before the door slams me on the ass. No good deed ever goes unpunished. Wonder who said it first?*

The pilot looked over at me and said "You said you were a pilot?"

"Yeah, haven't flown a 185 since last spring when our herring pilot checked me out on one." Dog and I had a fun day. These birds are real sportscars!

Pilot said "That's OK I'll mostly just need your muscles to help me overcome this trim." For the survey he had trimmed the 185 for slow flight, about 65 mph as I recall. "Unlock that set of dual controls you have."

I bent down to reach the rudder pedals locked against the floor in front of my seat. The pilot continued to repeat spinning the trim control trying to break the ice. Rudder pedals popped up under my feet as I freed them. Next, I reached forward to pull the pin locking the copilot's yoke against the instrument panel. Red faced from effort the pilot spun the trim tab wheel again.

"Controls are free." I said. Lord thank you for a wonderful life and wife. Please see to it she's cared for after I'm gone. Thanks, may not be time to pray again.

How did the guy planning not to fly anymore surveys and retire end up in a plane with frozen trim tabs? After cheating death that July day in 1994 I did check with Marsha who was all ready for me to retire. Eleven years in Bethel were enough, she wanted a change. Personnel explained my twenty years wasn't actually up until October. I had been including the seasonal time I had "purchased." Turns out that didn't count towards completing your twenty, it just increased your benefit since that was calculated based on your months of service.

Went home and explained it all to Marsha. Since we didn't have a clear idea of our retirement plan, we chose a flexible one, we would buy a pickup and travel trailer and live on the road until we found paradise. Ordering the truck and trailer meant we couldn't pick them up in Anchorage until the next spring. Besides we had to sell the house and when I took over my predecessor had left a draft annual report that had been rejected by the region. Staff and I had to rewrite virtually the whole thing. I didn't want to do that to whoever followed me so we finally decided on April 30, 1995 as my last day. We were busy with reducing our household, the state paid for our move, up to $5,000, to Bethel but retirees didn't get a final move back to the point of transfer.

At work, staff and I were busy writing, proof reading, correcting and reproofing the annual management report. In addition to our regular tasks. I wanted the AMR to be perfect. Our detailed proofreading discovered some mistakes that had been carried forward for years, which probably proved they weren't important enough to bother with but we did anyway. It was actually fun going back to the old AMRs from the sixties to find the correct numbers. I hadn't looked at most of those old reports since I took over in 1984. I had read them all in order to learn my new job.

March had a series of storms that seemed to make outdoor recreation unpleasant to impossible. As my last month approached, I was guilty of enjoying the Wildlife biologist's growing concern that he wasn't going to get the muskox count on Nunivak Island done before the snow melted due to bad survey weather. Finally, the weather broke, an Arctic high moved in from Siberia. Flying conditions were CAVU, temperatures were in the minus twenty to thirty range, the air was dry, still and dense (The colder the air is the less humidity it can hold and the denser it becomes which improves flying.).

Randy, the Wildlife biologist, came into my office "Kim this weather is only going to hold for a couple of days. FWS and I are going to team-up to get the muskox and reindeer survey done on Nunivak. They're bringing a plane and pilot down from Fairbanks. We'll have enough planes to divide up the island and get it all done in one day. But" *Here it comes.* "we're short one observer. Can you help out.

"Sure, I've been getting office fever, getting out will be good. You sure a fish counter can tell a muskox from a reindeer?"

"Great I'll get your maps and brief you for tomorrow."

Made Randy happy. Nunivak isn't mountainous so flying transects for critters should be a nice safe survey. He didn't answer my question or laugh. Guess he thinks I know the difference.

"Here I'll show you what we're doing and let you pick which area you want to do." Randy said returning from his office with a clipboard and photocopies of topo maps. We huddled.

Nunivak Island has a reindeer herd that is free ranging but owned by the Mekoryuk Village Corporation. They have a grazing lease with the USFWS that allows the reindeer on the Yukon Delta Refuge lands on Nunivak. Which is why FWS needed a count, since Mekoryuk had exceeded the number of animals allowed under the lease when their butchering plant burned down. As a result, they were only harvesting antlers in velvet for the Asian medicinal market. The antler harvest required rounding up the deer and herding them through a chute with a squeeze box. A couple of clips with a bolt cutter and rhe reindeer was free to grow another set for next year. The small number of reindeer shot by the villagers didn't match the birth rate of the herd so it continued to grow. While Mekoryuk navigated the process of replacing the plant they began selling reindeer hunts to nonislanders tring to control the herd. FWS needed to find out if the herd still exceeded the number allowed in the lease. In which case, they would require culling the herd during the antler harvest.

Randy needed the muskox survey since the drawing hunt for muskox was how the Department prevented their overpopulation and starvation. At that time, it was the only muskox hunt in the US so was a big draw and economically important to the Mekoryuk and Delta.

The pilot (I'm sorry I've forgotten your name.) and I hit it off and had a pleasant flight out exchanging stories. Then we set to work on the South-Central area of Nunivak that I had chosen. The coast along there is mostly huge beaches, good emergency landing spots. With the perfect survey conditions, we got done early so we radioed Randy in his plane. He radioed back asking if we could do the west coast sector. We had enough fuel so went for it. As we completed the cliff bound west coast, we found ourselves needing to refuel at Mekoryuk before returning to Bethel. That's when we discovered the plane was frozen in a nose-high slow flight configuration.

With my set of controls unlocked, the pilot and I began rehearsing a landing procedure that included my extra muscle to perform a landing. If anyone was watching they probably thought the plane "landing" at 1500' was being flown by madmen. Our main problem was with the plane trimmed for slow flight it was difficult to "flare", that is raise the nose to stall the plane. Yes, I know that sounds a little counter intuitive, I mean if your trimmed nose high for slow flight then all you need to do is raise it a little higher and you flared the plane. Trimmed for slow flight, the plane was almost already flared so there wasn't much elevator left to raise the nose higher. Slow flight is to avoid stalling at slow speed. The tail was so low in this configuration it would hit the ground before the main gear, probably bending or breaking the plane in half if you cut power. To do a wheel landing, you had to force the nose down through the nose high attitude to level. That's where my extra muscle came in. Our practice showed that the two of us could force the nose down so we could make a tail high wheel landing. I was amazed and frightened how much force it took to adjust the plane's attitude even with the engine throttled down.

With Mekoryuk, in sight the pilot announced an emergency landing for any approaching traffic and whatever meager rescue effort might be available. Mekoryuk is an uncontrolled airport and the village is too small to have any medical services except a village health aid.

Emergency landing. Being wrapped in an aluminum skin bleeding at 20 below. Guess we won't suffer long. Lord forgive my sins and thank you for an exciting life. This last part is getting a little too exciting. Shouldn't pray that.

Doesn't matter he knew what you were thinking. Is God a he? Hey, your about to die if you screwup pay attention. Right.

My distracted thoughts were interrupted by Tom Ratlidge's (Sorry Tom not sure about the spelling.) gruff voice "Heard your emergency. What's wrong."

"Trim tabs are frozen but we've been rehearsing at altitude, I think we got this landing."

After a thoughtful silence, Tom came back "Crank that tab control back as far as it goes, then spin it back as hard and fast as you can."

"Already tried that, repeatedly but once more won't hurt." While speaking the pilot had been backing up the trim tab wheel back as far as it would go, then hard and fast he spun it into the stoppage. There was a small "crack" as it reached the stop. He was then able to adjust trim to normal cruise.

WE'RE SAVED!

"Thanks, it worked, finally. We're good. Going to land for gas, then return to Bethel."

"Randy wants to know if you finished the count."

I told the pilot through my headset "Yep were done. Unless he has an unsurveyed block "*Please* be done.

The pilot repeated my answer back over the air. Dual headsets are kind of weird you can talk to each other and hear everything on the radio but only the pilot can broadcast.

Tom came back "Randy's celebrating, the island is done. Out."

We landed safely. A reminder of what almost happened lay to one side of the runway. The wrecked hulk of a plane that crash landed at Nunivak after exhausting its fuel. My pilot asked about it and I answered; "Missionary and his family flew to Siberia to save the communists. Story goes the Soviets held them for a couple days then let them go. They got lost in fog over Bering Sea and found Mekoryuk just as they ran out of gas. Guess it was a good landing everyone walked away."

The pilot held the nozzle into the gas tank up on the wing, I was below hand pumping the aviation gas out of a 55-gallon drum. "Doesn't look like a good landing to me. Who was the guy who helped on the radio?" The pilot asked.

"Tom Ratlidge, he's chief pilot and part owner of Executive Air in Bethel. I think his voice is just naturally gruff. He's really a great guy and pilot but because of his last name he has the unfortunate nick name of Ratman."

"Well, he sure knows planes."

The trip home didn't have as much chatter as the trip out. I was kind of thoughtful. *OK, got the message. Time to* retire. Thanks.

OTHER BOOKS BY THIS AUTHOR
ALIBI MIKE and His Gang of Parasites on the State
METAMORPHOSIS

www.ingramcontent.com/pod-product-compliance
Lightning Source LLC
Chambersburg PA
CBHW051156120626
46547CB00012B/1080